Brain Compatible Strategies

BRAIN COMPATIBLE STRATEGIES

©1997 The Brain Store™, Inc.

Cover art, editing & layout: Melissa Fraser

The Brain Store™, Inc.
4202 Sorrento Valley Blvd., Ste. B • San Diego, CA 92121
phone: (800) 325-4769 • fax: (858) 546-7560
www.thebrainstore.com • email: info@thebrainstore.com

Printed in the United States of America
Published by The Brain Store™, Inc.
San Diego, CA, USA

ISBN #0-9637832-7-0

Preface

"I know that the brain is important. But I'm a practical person. Have you got something I can start using tomorrow?" My response is usually, "Almost any activity can be brain-compatible, if it's done right."

"Could you give me a few examples?" I'm often asked. Well, I realize it's probably more a function of differences in learning styles than anything else. Nearly any activity can be good for the brain. In fact, it's harder to find something that is not "brain-based" than something that is. But because I have been asked so many times for "the best brain-based ones," here you are.

I decided to research specific activities that are not just "fun to do," but those that have direct research-proven links. In this book, you'll get great strategies that stimulate neural growth as well as the ones that are the fast-track towards better learning. This book provides simple, user-friendly activities based on the many practical principles of neuroscience.

This book is designed to be a fun-filled starter for you. But it is not all fun and games. Building a better brain is critical to the lifelong learning process. Yet, I have purposely not included a technical explanation of each activity. Nor have I provided the citations in the copy. For more of the theory and research on each of these topics, please refer to the resources listed in the back of the book. I think that will make the book much more readable.

These ideas will work because they are based on the way our brain actually works and the way real people actually learn. Good luck and enjoy the process.

How To Use This Book

No one single activity is going to turn a learner into an Albert Einstein, Quincy Jones or Martha Graham. That's why I suggest you take these activities and use them only as part of a larger program of learning enrichment. Expect to get small, consistent and purposeful improvements. And while it's true that each of these were selected for a reason, you must still use the broader fundamentals of brain-compatible learning in concert with these suggestions. Those principles include:

- absence of threat
- respecting uniqueness of learners
- engagement of emotions
- understanding brain's attention span
- active, relevant choice-driven learning

- complex, real-life learning
- eating proper foods
- specific, immediate feedback
- utilization of patterns in learning
- engagement of meaning

Our brain has "windows of opportunity" for learning particular subjects and skills, so not every suggestion can be optimal at every age. That's why these suggestions are purposely diverse; some are for parents, some are for teachers, and some are for adult learners. Even within an age group, learners are different, so once again it helps to have a wide variety of suggestions.

Using the book is easy. Browse it and mark one or two ideas you'd like to start using and put them into practice. If an activity seems like a poor fit for your student, relax. Often you'll discover that, with a simple twist, the suggestion will work for your particular group. Feel free to adapt any idea your way.

You'll soon find that your learners are becoming more motivated, understanding things better, enjoying the learning process more, recalling the material better, and applying what they've learned in the real world. Over a year's time, by using one to two suggestions per week, you can expect the impact to be enormous.

The lower section of each page is for you ("I tried which ideas today"). Jot down your reaction to the suggestions. Or, jot down the next time you plan to use the idea, or later, you might even record what the results were or what you plan to do differently next time. Feel free to write in this book–that's part of the learning process. This book is user-friendly and hopefully, quite valuable. Have fun with it!

Table of Contents

Benefits of Brain Compatible Strategies:

- Skyrocket Memory
- Improve Intrinsic Motivation
- Help Create Meaning
- Build Lifelong Learners
- Instill Key Learning Skills
- Boost Attention Levels
- Build Self-Esteem

Brain
Compatible
Strategies

Smart Activators for the Auditory Cortex

For optimal learning it's critical to stimulate the auditory cortex of the brain. The better this area develops early in life the fewer problems you'll find later on. Whether it's learning to read, speech, balance, posture or coordination, stimulating this area of the brain is crucial to development. Research suggests that many kinds of sounds and combined activities are good for the brain.

Suggestions

✔ **Repetition.** It's good for the brain, but the old "drill and kill" is outdated. It makes more sense to "drill and thrill." Make the repetition interesting, relevant and challenging. Repeat key ideas with a twist, repeat songs in a new way, repeat rituals and repeat good habits.

✔ **Singing songs.** Usually the easiest place to do this is K-2 or a school choir. But also sing school songs, re-do a pop song with new lyrics or re-write the lyrics to childhood songs and sing those as a content review.

✔ **Active listening.** Instead of using music as background, ask students to actively listen to Mozart Piano Sonatas in D Major for 5-10 minutes daily. Then follow that up with tasks involving abstract and spatial reasoning.

✔ **Playing & making music.** Bring instruments to class. Allow students to bring them to class. Express ideas through music for a few minutes a day. Do "period music" so students can learn how music was composed in other times in history.

✔ **Sensory awareness.** Ask students to move slowly from one side of the room to another and identify all the senses as they go. Do closed-eye listening and sound identification while sitting for three minutes. When done, write out what was heard. How many different sounds can you identify?

I tried which ideas today? What were the results?
What will I do differently next time?

_____

_____

_____

Childhood Games are Good for the Brain

Surprisingly, many common games are good for the brain. The single, number one, all-time best activity for greater brain growth is problem-solving. The best problems to solve involve the following conditions. 1) They must be novel (change the content and process of the games often). 2) They must be challenging (make sure the difficulty level is appropriate). 3) They must be non-threatening (everyone can contribute), and stimulate emotions (anxiety, joy, anticipation, surprise and celebration). Can you use more games in your day?

Suggestions

There are many games that fit these criteria. For young learners, use games designed for them. For adolescent or adult learners, use these games as a template and customize them to create a new, content appropriate game.

✔ **Board game ideas:** (there are hundreds!) Monopoly, Round the world, Sale of the Century, Jeopardy, 20 Questions, the Game of Clue, Trivial Pursuit, Crossword, Spelling "baseball," Tic-tac-toe, Bingo, Snakes and Ladders, dominos, chess, hangman or Where in the World is Carmen San Diego?

✔ **Customized example:** With adolescents or adult learners, use Monopoly or Bingo as a review. Put the class in teams of four each. Give them 1 hour to substitute, alter and re-label either of the games to match the content of the course. The first try is usually a bit rough. But it's the process of doing it that's the win, not the slick polish of a final product. Once they have finished their version of the game, I let a team try it out on another team or with the class.

✔ **Elementary learners:** The games, just as they are, can be terrific for the brain. Challenging and novel problem-solving is the single best exercise for enriching our gray matter. But add variety–have the students work in pairs to cooperate on game strategy. Give them game consultants (other students, who seem to win too much!) or let them design minor variations in the game.

I tried which ideas today? What were the results?
What will I do differently next time?

_____

_____

_____

Greater Meaning from Multiple Contexts

When learning occurs, cells are stimulated to grow branch-like extensions called dendrites. Each dendrite provides another pathway with which connections can be made. What we call "greater depth of meaning" simply means cells making more connections and new pathways to other cells. The secret for you is to provide multiple contexts for learning the same thing. That means the more ways we learn something, in more situations, with more intelligences, more emotions, more forms of media, the better. This allows us to access what was learned far easier, much later on.

Suggestions

✔ Design learning a topic in several different ways. Encourage peer teaching, the use of computers, mind-maps and personal investigation.

✔ Encourage greater group work. Make sure they get at least one chance per day to interact as a group.

✔ Use guest speakers, field trips and video more often. This creates greater diversity of learning.

✔ Bring up personal examples (yours & theirs) through discussion or group work. Ask students to do a variation of what you did in class, at home (make sure it's fun!).

✔ Use sports events, home, outside recreation areas and other locations for learning. Even the journey on the way to class can become a place to learn.

I tried which ideas today? What were the results?
What will I do differently next time?

_____

_____

_____

Specific Feedback Accelerates Learning

One of the best ways to boost learning is to dramatically increase the quantity and quality of feedback. The brain is a complex organ that thrives on information and corrections that allow it to be better at learning and survival behaviors. For growing greater dendrites in the brain, increased feedback is king. In some college and university classrooms, learners are asked to go months at a time without feedback! Often a professor will use just a mid-term and final for evaluating progress. Make it your personal and professional promise to give your students some kind of feedback within any 30 minute time frame. In the old model of the presenter providing all the feedback, it's impossible. One presenter for 35 kids, and the ratio doesn't work out. Fortunately, it can come from many sources besides you.

Suggestions

✔ Provide ways that students can find answers to their work through self-correction. For instance, tests and quizzes graded on the spot.

✔ Student set daily or weekly goals, using checklists or timelines. Then let them check themselves against that list.

✔ Allow students to work in groups and teams to teach each other, so that each learner can get immediate feedback from peers. Students write a summary of the class topic in one page or less, divide into teams, and read each other's summaries.

✔ Help students design a performance or grading rubric. Use far more student self-assessment so that learners can evaluate themselves and know exactly how they are doing.

✔ Create rituals that provide feedback. This gives the students "permission" to interact and improve themselves. An example is after each assignment, peers assess each other and give each other either a high five or "thanks!"

I tried which ideas today? What were the results?
What will I do differently next time?

_____

_____

_____

Musical Chairs for Both Fun and Learning

So many of the games from our childhood may seem silly, but with a few twists, they can great for the brain and overall learning.

Suggestions

Have everyone gather in a circle, with 1 person per chair. Once the game starts, you quickly remove one of the chairs, pulling it outside the circle and setting it away. To start the game, you ask all to stand up and do something easy and fun to others (like introduce yourself, give positive affirmations, say one thing you've learned today, find others with a birthday in your same month or year, or shaking hands a new way, etc.).

Meanwhile, you're standing outside the circle, playing fun, loud music. When you stop the music (after about 5-20 seconds), everyone runs for a chair. But there's not enough! The one left standing is the new "music master." He gets to start and stop the music (like you just did). But first, he has to show he's worthy by doing some activity (see below).

You can use this game to do almost any appropriate activity. It's critical to keep it non-threatening. The person left standing must be able to do what you ask him to do AND it must not be anything embarrassing. That's why it's good to let people have time for preparation or reflection before you start the game. Use the game for:

✔ **Get to know you activity**–they must introduce three others.
✔ **Review activity**–they must state one or two things learned.
✔ **Self-disclosure activity**–they must share something about themselves that others might not know.
✔ **Storytelling**–they must continue a story that was started earlier.
✔ **Concept connecting**–they must connect one idea to another.

I tried which ideas today? What were the results?
What will I do differently next time?

_____

_____

_____

Learning With Feelings

Research suggests that feelings are critical to the learning process in many ways. Our feelings help us determine: 1) If we want to learn a subject, 2) how we feel about a subject, 3) whether we want to learn about a subject, 4) if we believe the information is true, and 5) how long we remember the information.

Your learners can understand a topic without having feelings about it, but it won't mean anything to them until an emotion is attached to it. It simply is not real to the brain until we "feel" it is real. Learning without feelings is incomplete. One top researcher said, "Our brain is just a box packed with emotions." Another said, "Think of the brain *not* as a computer, but a gland!" How can you integrate emotions more productively into the learning process?

Suggestions

✔ Put learners into a positive state before learning. Activate their curiosity, past feelings of success or anticipation about future fun.

✔ Actively engage emotions while learning. Use drama, storytelling, music and/or movement. Read a story using a movie soundtrack, classical (Beethoven) or romantic (Flight of the bumblebee?) music. Ask students to act out the learning by making a commercial for the material.

✔ Use intense intellectual or physical activities (debates, student presentations, humor, or tug-o-war). Ask students to pick a partner, and a side of an argument. They get 60 seconds to argue their point of view as best they can, then they switch sides.

✔ Role model expression of emotions with poignant personal examples. The more you show that emotions can be strong, but appropriate, the safer you help make it for students to express them.

✔ Use rituals of celebration after completion of learning. This could include hi-fives, Olympic music, "show & tell" or (non-reward) fun certificates.

I tried which ideas today? What were the results?
What will I do differently next time?

_____

_____

_____

Ways Out of the Sacred "Learning Box"

The brain craves stimulation, change and novelty. Unfortunately, many teachers and trainers also crave control and predictability. As a result, you have classes and seminars that stay in the same "sacred box" (the classroom or training room) day after day.

You'd be surprised how easy it is to wake up the brain to fresh air (even if it's for two minutes). Go to novel locations and invigorate the thinking and learning.

Suggestions

✔ Ask everyone to pair up. Give them a "pair-share" activity and ask them to go for a walk outside (or in the building) if weather permits.

✔ Trade rooms with another presenter or teacher for an hour or a day. New stimulation, novel locations and fresh ideas may be great for bringing your subject to life.

✔ Do a "walking class." Take your group for a walk outside if weather permits, and continue to teach as you walk along. Trigger ideas related to the walk. For example, use shapes of the building to talk about mathematics, style of architecture to talk about history or culture and tie-in motivation and vision to the construction itself.

I tried which ideas today? What were the results?
What will I do differently next time?

_____

_____

_____

Dealing with Barriers to Learning

The brain has cells called neurons. Each cell can communicate with other cells to create connections. The chemicals that make these connections happen are called neurotransmitters. They act either to excite or inhibit cell interaction. It's like a lock and key arrangement where as long as the "keys" fit the receptor sites and you have more excitatory neurotransmitters than inhibitors, you'll you get a connection.

If our memories have strongly negative emotional content, they may activate inhibitory neurotransmitters. They act like closed venetian blinds to resist neuro-transmitters and hence, new learning. We've all heard of a "math block" or a foreign language block. The secret to dealing with these barriers is to recognize them and approach learning through other, more open channels.

Suggestions

✔ Make a list of the barriers your learners might have in the areas that impact you, like content (mathphobia or languages) or process ("Learning is way too hard work, I can't ever do it.")

✔ Create & post colorful peripheral posters that can influence them (Math is E-Z and Fun!, Learning Can Be Easy, I Can Learn Anything).

✔ Make the learning a by-product of another activity. Learn math by playing Bingo, quiz show, or by restoring an apartment. Learn languages by going to a restaurant, traveling, or watching a video with subtitles.

✔ Challenge learners to prove their own negative beliefs wrong. Ask them to create a list of reasons *why* their beliefs might be wrong, *what* they'll do about it and *when* they'll start.

✔ Provide optional resources, opportunities, and pathways to learn, using the multiple intelligences. For example, a new software to learn math, or travel to learn languages.

I tried which ideas today? What were the results?
What will I do differently next time?

_____

_____

_____

Hollywood Here I Come...Role-Play

When your students do role-play, several good things happen. The kinesthetic part of us gets involved in the role-play, and engages emotions, builds problem-solving and aids learning by encapsulating it more easily in the brain so it can be recalled later. Here are some "theater" games you can use with almost any group. Simply decide which idea is most appropriate and when.

Suggestions

✔ **Ad-ons.** It's a fun way to review. Invite one person to come up to the front of the room and act out or posture something that they have learned. Others come up and join the impromptu living sculpture until you have one giant human scenario of they've been learning.

✔ **Body machines.** Role-play how a machine (or customer service, or car, barcode, computer, etc.) works. This activity is best when all work as a team.

✔ **Body talk.** Use as an ice-breaker. A person comes up front and demonstrates something they can do with their body (keep it clean!), like double jointed-ness, rolling the tongue, a handspring, etc.

✔ **Commercial breaks.** A great way to review. Each team (or pair) is assigned a topic or they choose one. After ten minutes of rehearsal, teams offer an impromptu TV commercial break. They get 30" using the material that they've been learning... It can be fun, bizarre, cute, etc. Their goal is to get us to *want* to buy a service or a product from them.

I tried which ideas today? What were the results?
What will I do differently next time?

_____

_____

_____

Learn Best by De-Briefing Failures

Learning comes in many forms. We learn basic concepts (implicit knowledge, we just "know") from doing an activity and describing what we learn. Research suggests that human subjects learned declarative knowledge (explicit strategies that can be shared with another) from unsuccessful performances. In other words, doing it right the first time produced no new learning. But failing at it gets us to become more of a "student of learning."

Failure, can indeed be, a great strategy. Second, the fine tuning comes from doing it over and over (with specific feedback), not just talking about it. Third, these two types of knowledge can develop at the same time. And last, subjects often said they were "clueless" and did not know what to do only four to six trials ahead of their breakthroughs.

Suggestions

✔ During motor learning, ask participants to verbalize what they are doing while they do it. Have them work with a partner to increase accountability.

✔ While keeping feedback high, provide sufficient time to learn from the mistakes. Often a breakthrough is just around the corner. Tell students that it's OK to fail, over and over.

✔ Help others understand the two types of learning (both "body-knowing" and the ability to explain it) and make it a goal to end up with both.

I tried which ideas today? What were the results?
What will I *do* differently next time?

_____

_____

_____

Use Integrated, In-Context Curriculum

The brain learns best in a real-word immersion of learning (going to a county fair, renting an apartment, publishing a magazine, visiting a retirement community, riding a bike). It learns poorly when we break the information to be learned into micro-chunks and learn them one small piece or topic at a time. Imagine learning to ride a bicycle by taking classes in mechanics, road safety, neighborhood geography, social structure, first aid and courage. We'd never even want to try it and we certainly wouldn't enjoy the process. Instead, most of us just jumped on a bicycle and tried it out. In the classroom, make learning as real-world as possible.

Suggestions

✔ Pick a single theme to use for several months, one that has many opportunities to break off into other sub-topics. Topics like "change" or "shapes" or "growing" or "perspectives."

✔ In math it can be as simple as running a lemonade stand to somthing as complex as a real estate finance, purchase & renovation. In literature, it can be a universal work that triggers many other paths. In geography, it might be planning an around-the-world trip. In languages, it might be creating comic books or tourist guides in the topic language or becoming interpreters for immigrants.

✔ Provide choice for the learners so that they can go in one of several directions. That way they can pick something relevant to them.

✔ Stay with that theme topic, but go off on interdisciplinary tangents, just like real life. For example, studying a river can mean learning about it's history, geography, ecology, cultures, etc.

✔ Provide the resources so learners can gain information from guest speakers, on-location sites, computers, group interaction and the media.

I tried which ideas today? What were the results?
What will I do differently next time?

_____

_____

_____

Use Ball Toss to Boost Thinking

Good games encourage problem-solving, cooperation, self-discovery and physical movement. Nearly any game, if done well, can be a "bright brain" game. Ball toss gives you and your students the ability to think quickly, in a safe environment, with novelty and fun.

The game is best with 5-6 students, standing in a 6-8 foot diameter circle, facing each other. The objects can be: a sock, a kooshball, a piece of fruit, a soft or hard-boiled egg, a stuffed animal, or a rubber ball. The rules are simple: 1) always "float" the pass to another person higher than their head. 2) you have the right to take your time to answer, but only talk when you have the object. 3) avoid the same consecutive answers. 4) no passing to the same person or the one next to you. Put on some light, quick, piano music (Mozart's Piano Sonata in D Major is excellent). When the game has been going for about 2 minutes, allow each group to change their rules for the next 2 minutes. 2 minutes later, allow them to change the rules again. The game is best run for about 6 minutes.

Suggestions

Here are some ways to use the game; it works with children, teens or adults. Just change the rules or the content of the game.

✔ **With children.** Start or continue a story, do spelling, give affirmations, give compliments, do problem-solving, I saw..., rhyming, math facts, names, places, capitols, presidents, personal examples, etc.

✔ **With adolescents.** Take opposing ideas on a topic, invent test questions, introduce yourself, review content, problem/solution, brainstorming.

✔ **With adults.** Give examples of customer service, brainstorming, tell factual story or company history, give new vocabulary for a job, problem/solution, explain the details of some topic (one sentence at a time), product development or improvements.

I tried which ideas today? What were the results?
What will I do differently next time?

_____

_____

_____

Let Learners Create Their Own Meaning

The brain thrives on meaning, not random information. But what makes things meaningful to your brain? Several things: 1) putting information together to make a pattern, to understand relationships and connections, 2) That which stimulates emotions, either positively or negatively, and 3) That which impacts the learner's personal life. Without meaning, learners lose interest and intrinsic motivation wanes. Although you can't make something meaningful for another, you can help encourage the development of meaning.

Suggestions

✔ Provide time to discuss the relevance in small groups or with partners. Graphic organizers or mind maps are also excellent.

✔ Purposely engage emotions in the process of learning by making the material sad, suspenseful, or dramatic. Use celebrations, debates, music, role-play or theater to evoke emotions.

✔ Tie the learning into closely held personal values of the learners: security (younger learners and seniors) peer acceptance and identity (adolescents), autonomy (young adults), respect and achievement (adults). Do this through discussion, mapping or current events.

✔ Ask learners to find three ways it can relate to their own lives. It might be through travel they've done, a TV show they watched, etc.

✔ Allow reflection time and journal writing on the topic. Encourage your students to be personal and go into some detail.

I tried which ideas today? What were the results?
What will I do differently next time?

_____
_____
_____

Cross Laterals "Unstick" Learning

When learners get stuck, it usually has one of two forms. The "left brain stuck" is an analytical quagmire. He says, "I tried everything; I did this, I did that and I just can't seem to find my way out of it." The "right brain stuck" is just overwhelm; you ask, "Where are you stuck?" She answers, "Everywhere! I'm just hopelessly lost!"

There is some help. The brain is most effective at problem-solving when it is using both sides of the brain. During the day, hormonal fluctuations trigger stronger blood flows to different sides of the brain during the day. It's actually normal for an alternation of left-to-right-to-left again brain dominance. You want to encourage the use of both sides of the brain for best learning. The right side of the brain controls the left side of the body. Conversely, the left side of the brain controls the right side of the body. Activities which are "cross-lateral" are great at forcing the brain to "talk to itself" and use both hemispheres. The purpose is to activate the brain through movement.

Suggestions

✔ Touch hands to opposite knees (do this about 10 times).
✔ Give yourself a pat on the back on the opposite side.
✔ Touch opposite hips, opposite elbows, opposite heels.
✔ Do air swimming – one arm in one direction of freestyle and the other arm swimming in the other direction.
✔ Touch nose and hold opposite ear then switch hands three times.
✔ Do "sideways 8s" in front of you by tracing the pattern of the number eight with your thumb ups sign...start your 8 at the center, arms length, going up and to the left, do big loops on both sides and switch sides. Follow with your eyes and repeat pattern three times, switch hands. Then do the pattern with both hands.

I tried which ideas today? What were the results?
What will I do differently next time?

_____

_____

_____

Use More Questions Than Answers

When it comes to learning, the brain is more receptive to questions than answers. Why? It seems that two things occur: 1) curiosity is a distinct physiological state. It triggers changes in our posture, eye movements and promotes the chemical reactions that are advantageous to better arousal, learning and recall 2) when we ask a question of ourselves, the brain will continue to process it even after we have come up with an answer. To your brain, the process is far more important than the answer!

In short, there's an increase in capability when learning with questions and a "coasting release" with the brain as the answers are found. This may explain why some laboratory or theoretical scientist can remain dedicated in pursuit of a specific solution for years. The quest is far more powerful than the answer.

Suggestions

✔ Allow students to generate questions in advance of a topic. They can post them up or publish them or put them on tape.

✔ You (or your students) write up questions and put them in a hat or a basket. Have daily "drawings" for the group. Students can vote on the best or most thought provoking questions.

✔ Trade questions with other teachers. Bring in them from home; have parents questions. Have a "question of the day" board with contributions by you or the students.

✔ Students write up their own questions for the tests.

✔ Encourage questions. Give clear, thoughtful answers. Turn questions into interesting divergent paths of exploration.

I tried which ideas today? What were the results?
What will I do differently next time?

_____

_____

_____

Get Mental & Physical Boosts

Many of the traditional games were designed for pure physical fun. Nothing wrong with that. But let's add a little spice to them and get our brain involved. It makes the game a bit more challenging and it can serve the double purpose of a review (or ?).

Suggestions

✔ **Touch & Go.** Students get up, in sequence, touch 5 pieces of gold, 4 pieces of silver, 3 of glass, 2 of leather, 1 of clothing label on someone else. All items must be at least 10 or more feet apart. Variations w/content: Math: touch right angles, cylinders, cubes, rectangles, length, height. Science: touch textures, colors, weights, rarity, solids. History: touch things that fit a certain time era, things which could be used to... English: touch objects which could be used to... make a sentence, have double meanings, capitalized. Economics: touch items in order of value, cost. Use colors!

✔ **Circle "run-ons".** All stand up in their own groups or teams, facing the group leader. The audience is given a topic for review. The group leader starts a sentence on the topic and leaves it hanging (such as "Energizers are best for..."). The person to his or her left (or right, or whomever's chosen), continues the "run-on" sentence, but again, leaves it hanging for the next person. The goal is to keep the sentence going for as long as you can. The one who ends the sentence gets a big groan from the others, but gets to start a new sentence. Add variety, like the circle has to be moving while talking. Or, someone stands on one leg until their turn.

I tried which ideas today? What were the results?
What will I *do* differently next time?

_____

_____

_____

How to Engage the Spatial-Episodic Memory

Your brain has two parallel visual systems. The impact of this is that every-thing you see is recorded as what (content), and where (context). That means your brain sorts incoming data based on whether it is "embedded" in content or "embedded" in context. Read a paragraph on gardening out of a book; the information is content within content. Or, go out to your garden and follow the directions on the back of the seed package and plant some flowers. Both are ways to learn, but one way, the second, is more memorable.

That's because all learning is, in some way, contextually embedded. But the more similar the context for the learning to other contexts, the harder it is for the brain to retrieve that information (imagine having all your computer files named the same!). The location and circumstances provide the brain many more identifying clues for better retrieval. The more you utilize this spatial-episodic memory, the greater the recall of your learners. Context provides dozens of sen-sory cues that can better trigger memory and recall later.

Suggestions

✔ Change the locations of learning, go outdoors, on field trips, or just switch rooms with another presenter for a day.

✔ Bring in guest speakers (they could be from your own school) to change the circumstances of the class.

✔ Use props, costumes and special music. The best props are the ones the students wear, not what you wear. Have a big prop box in the back of the room.

✔ Change the seating, work in pairs, teams, new groups, or on the floor.

✔ Create special events, themes, occasions to "anchor" the learning. Use holidays, seasons, colors, etc.

I tried which ideas today? What were the results?
What will I do differently next time?

_____

_____

_____

Brain-Breaks, Everyone Needs Them

It's great to mix the intellectual with the physical. But sometimes, what is really needed is to let off some steam and simply energize the group with some activity. Here's four you might like.

Suggestions

✔ **Clapping games.** You start a clap or rhythm, and students "pass" it around the room. Then the first student starts a clapping rhythm and others follow suit. Use a pattern, they listen and repeat the pattern. Good for memory and music skills.

✔ **Gordian knot.** Teams of 6 or 8 stand in a circle, facing each other, 2 feet apart. One reaches across with one hand and clasps the hand of another. Each person clasps the hand of the opposite person, so both hands are full. You now have everyone holding the opposite person's hand. Now, they have to untie themselves from this giant knot while still keeping hands clasped.

✔ **Lap sit.** Good for your whole group... all stand in a circle, facing the back of the person in front of you, just six inches behind the person in front, hold on to their waist and all gently sit down on person's lap behind you... at the same time... it's fun!

✔ **Matching faces/matching sounds.** The group stands in a large circle. You or a student starts with a face or sound, then "passes" it. That means the person to their left repeats it and "passes it" again to their left...and so on...until all have done it and a new person starts up the cycle with a new face or sound. Variations...pass a face in one direction, a sound in the other direction...pass a gesture, an action, etc.

I tried which ideas today? What were the results?
What will I do differently next time?

_____

_____

_____

Visuals and Peripherals Impact Learning

The human brain can normally register over 36,000 images per hour. The eyes are designed to take in 30 million bits of information per second. In the learning context, it makes sense to take advantage of this amazing organ that is hungry for pictures, movies and images. But, most of what the brain learns is nonconscious. In fact, studies done on the impact of peripherals (posters, pictures, drawings, symbols) suggest they are much more powerful influences on the brain than previously thought. After two weeks, the effects of direct instruction have diminished. But the effects of peripherals often go up!

Suggestions

✔ Use colorful, symbolic posters to inspire (reaching top of mountain, working as a team, exciting discoveries, great people in history, etc.). Ask students to find these and bring them in, or make them.

✔ Use course preview information, graphically organized as a poster. Make it into a mindmap and have them copy it.

✔ Post student work from teams, not individuals.

✔ Put up affirmations for learners ("Your success is assured"). Ask them to create their own positive messages.

✔ Ask students to make murals, mindscapes or "positive" graffiti for the walls of the room. They can create course posters that not only help them review, but build relationships with others in the process.

✔ While talking, use more overhead transparencies, flip charts, pictures or have students bring them. Have two students, one on each side of the chalkboard (or at a flip chart etc.) actually mind map what you are saying while you are saying it. Create a continuous graphic organized record of class presentations. Rotate kids.

✔ Use videos to enhance learning.

**I tried which ideas today? What were the results?
What will I do differently next time?**

_____

_____

_____

The Real Power of Music

Brain research out of the University of California at Irvine tells us two important new things about the brain. First, music can charge and energize our brain. When music harmonizes with our own rhythms, we feel energized by it. Some research suggests our brain gains energy from certain frequencies (about 8,000 Hz). Specially selected music has been found to have a powerful energizing influence on the brain.

Another effect is boosting intelligence. Certain Mozart compositions (Piano Sonata in D Major) have helped learners raise their intelligence scores on spatial-temporal reasoning after just ten minutes of listening. The effect does not last, but it can be reactivated at any time. When music runs counter to our own natural frequency rhythms, (like heavy metal) we can feel irritated and stressed.

Suggestions

✔ Play positive energizing music before the start of class. You might use movie themes.
✔ Play specific compositions in moments of emotional highs (trumpets, fanfare, Olympics music, Rocky, Hallelujah Chorus, etc.).
✔ Play special Romantic or Classical selections for dramatic prose or for concert readings (Beethoven's Piano concerto #1, Symphony Fantastique by Berlioz, etc.).
✔ Play low volume background baroque to soothe, calm & relax (Handel's Water Music, Four Seasons by Vivaldi, Bach's Brandenburg Concertos).
✔ Play Mozart's Piano Sonata in D Major before tasks involving spatial temporal reasoning (assembling objects, building, puzzles or mindmapping).
✔ Play special music selections to close class (Wonderful World, I've Had the Time of My Life, Happy Trails, Simply the Best, etc.).

I tried which ideas today? What were the results?
What will I do differently next time?

_____

_____

_____

Breaking Monotony with Novelty and Fun

We all like some things be predictable. That gives us some peace of mind. Too much predictability and you get bored. How can you prevent that? Here are a few ways to add to your toolbox.

Suggestions

✔ **Humor break.** Everyone stands up and closes their eyes. Those that can think of a recent or old joke, raises their hand. Everyone opens their eyes. Those with their hands still down cluster around someone who raised their hand. They tell the joke and get a round of applause, then everyone switches groups and joke tellers.

✔ **Pair (not peer) Teaching.** Everyone prepares a one minute review talk with a partner. The topic is something they've learned in the last hour. All students by random, numbers or volunteer, come up front to teach the whole group, with their partner, two at a time. Or, each pair that finishes gets to pick the next pair. Remember to assign a student timekeeper to insure they use the full minute, but no more.

✔ **A new place in space.** Every class day, each team or individual changes locations. You can do it to music, or do a rotation by quadrant or just change places with another. Whatever works! Everyone gets up and moves to a new place in the room. Or, ask the group to change the design of the room so that all the furniture is facing a new direction with a new front to the room.

I tried which ideas today? What were the results?
What will I do differently next time?

_____

_____

_____

Marching the Brain to Learning Success

Marching has some nice fringe benefits. It's obviously great for circulation and a breath of fresh air. But the rhythm can be great for learning, too. What's learned is more likely to be recalled later for three good reasons: 1) it's in the body, so it's kinesthetic learning 2) there's sounds and rhythms attached to it and 3) a change in locations triggers the spatial- episodic memory. Here's a few you might enjoy using.

Suggestions

✔ **Military March.** It's done the way recruits march around with a rhythmic chant. The base chorus is "It's real easy, see-say-do...we learned it first, and now you, too." Each person or team comes up with the alternating verses that are content reviews. Example: Chorus + "Memory is piece of cake, new locations make it rate, in a room or by the lake, e-motion will make it great" + chorus. After one team says their verse, the next team starts up. All teams repeat all the verses on the walk. Fun and healthy!

✔ **"Brain March."** Have students stand up and walk fast around the entire ground floor of the building just to get their circulation up. As a review, they are to tell ten others what they think has been the one, two or three keywords from the last half hour. Set a few rules first: safety, time, courtesy, noise, etc.

✔ **Follow the Leader.** Each team brainstorms a topic. Go for a walk. Use as a repetition memory game, perception or skills practice. A team or group leader takes their group with them. They act out or say something about the content, and the others follow along and repeat.

I tried which ideas today? What were the results?
What will I do differently next time?

_____

_____

_____

Add Good Stress, Eliminate Bad Stress

Research tells us that low to moderate stress is better for learning than no stress or high stress. It creates more resourceful and resilient lifelong learners. Good stress creates a moderate adrenaline rush, the type where you feel challenged to rise up to the occasion. Your best, resourceful alert states are evoked. Bad stress usually triggers an inappropriate amount of glutocorticoids into your system. This can be provoked by anxiety, induced learner helplessness or any perceived sense of threat. By evoking the right kind of stress and avoiding the bad stress, your learners are more likely to enjoy learning and be at their best.

Suggestions

✔ Provide the learners with the resources they need to succeed; too little and they stress out or feel helpless.

✔ Avoid inducing stress with irregular or unbeatable deadlines.

✔ Provide de-stressing time with relaxation or physical movement.

✔ Eliminate threats of negative consequences to students. This includes expressions such as, "If you do that one more time…!" or "You better quiet down and get ready to learn!"

✔ Encourage the appropriate expression of emotions to reduce stress. Use discussions, journaling, pair sharing or physical activity.

I tried which ideas today? What were the results?
What will I do differently next time?

_____

_____

_____

Problem-Solving Great for Growing Brains

The best exercise for the brain is good old-fashioned problem-solving. There are hundreds if not thousands of games that require focused concentration and problem-solving. Some of them have a specific objective, with others, the *process* is the value you want.

Suggestions

✔ **Hook and linking.** Games requiring matching words and definitions, likes and opposites are good. Have fun with scrabble, pictionary and pictogram games. How about a game of Squiggles, Concentration, I Spy, What's in the Box, Detective or What's Missing?

✔ **Listening games.** Chinese whispers, simon sez, I heard, telephone, cows, ducks.

✔ **Who and what am I?** Great to use as a review for a course. Put the key item for review (or a name or a place) on a piece of paper. When students enter, you tape or pin the item on their back. The students have to figure out what the item is by asking others in the room (who can see it) questions. All questions must be "yes or no" only.

✔ **Word puzzles.** Those are expressions or phrases that everyone knows. But they're formatted in an abbreviated way to make it a challenge to figure out. Give students several dozen to design on the subject you're learning. They design them, and test them out on other students. The one on the left below is "multiple intelligences." In the middle, it's "eggs, over easy," and last, "pizza with everything on it."

Intelligences	eggs	everything
Intelligences	easy	pizza
Intelligences		

I tried which ideas today? What were the results?
What will I do differently next time?

_____

_____

_____

Brain Learns Best with "Pulse" Learning Style

The human brain is not designed for continuous learning. That's because the brain needs processing time and "down time" away from directed, focused time. You can either have your learner's attention or they can be creating meaning, but you can't have both at once. The best learning occurs with alternating cycles of focus, diffusion, focus, diffusion. Focus learning is continued, directed attention with minimal learner choice. Examples include presenter lectures or active discussions. Diffusion is unfocused, positive choice time where the learner may be journaling, having partner discussions, using think time or doing projects.

The brain's natural and normal attention and learning process alternates from internal to external. It goes external to take in the information. It then goes internal to access memories and associations of events related to that information to make meaning out of it. This means that appropriate learning is more like an up-down or in-out cycle.

Suggestions

✔ Plan so that you have plenty of both kinds of activities.

✔ Keep focus activities short. You might focus for about the age of the learner in minutes, then diffuse for about 2-5 minutes. For a 10 year-old, focus for 10 minutes, then diffuse. Maximum of continuous focus time, for all ages, would be about 20 minutes.

✔ Allow students purposeful "down time" for several minutes a day with learner choice: mapping, reflection, journal writing or projects.

✔ If you see and hear too much diffusion or lack of focus among learners, use that as a reminder to change activities.

I tried which ideas today? What were the results?
What will I do differently next time?

_____

_____

_____

Motor Brain Activators

Are there fun activities that are good for developing learning skills? Definitely. The ones listed below are best for students age 3-8 years old. (Do each of these for two to five minutes. They'll take about 20 minutes to do each day. Continue for 22-26 weeks.

Suggestions

The trampoline and merry-go-round have all but been banned in schools around the world. Liability took priority over learning once again. But both of them happen to be very good for learning. Fortunately, there are variations you can use.

✔ **For trampoline,** use a "grape-stomping" exercise or hop-scotch games.
✔ **For merry-go-round,** use "Triangle Tag." It requires groups of four...three form a triangle, holding hands, the fourth stands outside the group and tries to tag whoever is "it"... the triangle team keeps spinning to avoid having the "it" person tagged! Fun!
✔ **Line and beam walking** are great for balance and the inner ear. These are easy to turn into games like "Birthday Wall." Give students a ledge or low wall (you can use a piece of tape or line, too) from six inches to two feet off the ground to use. Give the class a deadline (like one minute). Then ask them to line up, in order of their birthdays, from earliest in the year (Jan 1st?) to latest (Dec. 31st?). Put on fast music and let them all line up and balance (in order) in one minute.

I tried which ideas today? What were the results?
What will I do differently next time?

_____

_____

_____

Praise: Timing is Everything

What does brain research reveal about praise? What is the role of praise in a learning environment? Words do have an effect on the nervous system, our feelings and performance. They can raise our anxiety, negatively, if given before a task ("Diane, you are usually good in math, what's the answer to this question?..."). Diane may feel anxious and underperform. If the learner does not personally feel good about a task accomplished, praise (if in the eyes of the learner, seems undeserved) may lead to negative stored feelings, thus inhibiting future learning. The lessons?

Suggestions

✔ Allow the learner to help create the criteria for better self-assessment. Use the learner's own assessment often. It can be the first option for feedback. First, let students create and use their own criteria of quality in order to learn to give themselves feedback. Ask them what they thought of what they did.
✔ Make sure the feedback is specific and immediate.
✔ Praise after a task, not before it.
✔ Use extensive peer-generated praise.
✔ Contribute your personal opinion, feelings and specific feedback to the learner about the results of their action.

I tried which ideas today? What were the results?
What will I do differently next time?

_____

_____

_____

Review Quickies Good for Brain Boosting

It's frustrating for your students to learn so much, but have little to show for it the next day or at test time. Make it a daily habit to review material. How can you put together a fun way to review material? Here's a few ideas.

Suggestions

✔ **Frisbee review.** Whoever catches the Frisbee (or whatever object), says one thing that they've learned (or implications of it) from the last class session.

✔ **Poster potpourri.** Everyone stands up and finds a partner. Each person looks around the room and visually picks out two or three posters that they like. Each person takes their partner with them and walks over to the posters and tells their partner what hit home for them. Each explains why that one poster in particular was so meaningful to them.

✔ **Stand-up reviews.** Past content review, eyes closed or open, music or no music. Could be a "walking review" too. Also do pair-share with high-speed, quickie "word association" review. One says a word, the other says the first word that comes to mind on that topic.

✔ **I did it my way.** It's the use of music & song activities in a fun way. Write out the lyrics to a song and pass it out. Students revise and re-write lyrics using key things learned. Or, re-contextualize the use of a song. The audience can write brand new words to sing or act out and everyone participates.

I tried which ideas today? What were the results?
What will I do differently next time?

_____

_____

_____

Nonconscious Messages are Powerful

Research suggests that we react to information that is below conscious awareness. Our brain triggers reactions in pulse, perspiration and stress. How does this affect you? Your learners are picking up more information than you are consciously giving them. Top presenters understand congruency, the art of matching verbal and nonverbal messages. That's why taking acting lessons might be an important self-investment for presenters. You want to be sure to give the right message to the learner's brains. Over 99% of all learning is nonconscious. So, although your conscious mind can only process one sense at a time, on a nonconscious level, you are taking in many, many messages per second. Your learners may not be aware of most of the nonconscious learning they do, but you can be more aware of the messages you are sending.

Suggestions

✔ Purposely use tonal shifts, changes in pacing and volume, and gestures that add impact and drama to your teaching.
✔ Practice teaching or presenting in front of a mirror.
✔ Audio tape your class presentation and critique it.
✔ Take acting lessons at a local theater group, the Learning Annex, or a community college or university extension.
✔ Get more specific feedback from your learners on your intended messages.

I tried which ideas today? What were the results?
What will I do differently next time?

_____
_____
_____

When is as Important as What

Your own learners are strongly influenced by the body's internal clock when it comes to remembering what is learned. Why? The brain and body's biorhythms are strongly influenced by the periodic and natural release of hormones, including adrenaline, norepinephrine, testosterone, adrenaline, endorphins and vasopressin. Since memory is tied to our emotions and chemical balance, you get varying effects on learning.

In the morning, your brain seems to recall more literal, specific and detailed material. Males perform higher on spatial and gross motor in the morning while females do better on verbal and writing skills. The afternoon is reversed. For both sexes, midday may be better for easier, more repetitive learning. Afternoons and evening are better for relationships and more global understanding.

Suggestions

✔ Require minimal amounts of rote, useless recall questions.
✔ Provide learners with skills to develop their own memory.
✔ Make sure that with important content, emotions are engaged for better recall later.
✔ Allow more choice when learners are required to master something.
✔ Rotate your learning so that complex or new concepts are presented in the morning. Rotate with others.

I tried which ideas today? What were the results?
What will I do differently next time?

_____

_____

_____

Motor Brain Activators, Part II

Let's continue our listing of activities that are good for developing learning skills. The ones listed below are best for students ages 3-8 years old. (Do each of these for 2 to 5 minutes. They'll take about 20 minutes to do each day. Continue for 22-26 weeks.

Suggestions

✔ **Tracing, see-touch-trace activities.** These are great for developing the kinesthetic-spatial awareness skills. Allow students to locate a picture or drawing and trace it, first from the original, then from their tracing. Then let them pick an object, trace it onto paper and fill in the details.

✔ **Swinging and Rockerboards.** These are great for developing the inner ear, balance and reading skills. When outside, use a playground swing for 5 minutes. When inside, use a board (2 feet long and one foot wide) on a roller (like a rolling pin), and let students (with support) try to balance themselves.

✔ **Helicopter spinning.** Kids love to spin around, but there's more to it than just fun. It's great for the developing brain, too! Put on loud, upbeat music, and let kids spin in a circle (same direction) with their eyes closed (they'll get less dizzy and it does more good). Do this twice a day for 1 minute each.

✔ **Hopping, clapping, and rope-jump**. These activities are great for learning and the brain. Make sure you find ways to use them at least weekly.

✔ **Stirring**. Winding and using groove boards are great, too. Give kids something they can trace, stir, or follow in its tracks.

I tried which ideas today? What were the results?
What will I do differently next time?

_____

_____

_____

The Brain's Natural Learning Orientation

Biologically, the human brain is designed for survival through learning. But it is not at all designed for formal instruction. It makes sense to design your learning based on what the learners *perceive* they need to learn for social, physical and economic survival. Provide appropriate choice for your students to learn, and do not base it on instruction to "fill the learners up." That means no more "covering a topic." With practice, you'll switch from being a content-provider to becoming a catalyst of their learning.

Suggestions

✔ Allow students more control over their own learning.
✔ Get them involved in their own assessment criteria.
✔ Provide learning centers for them to learn at their own pace.
✔ Allow them to work more cooperatively and learn from each other.
✔ Design themes around what learners feel they need to learn, such as making social contact, developing autonomy, gaining security, making money, pleasing others, etc.

I tried which ideas today? What were the results?
What will I do differently next time?

_____

_____

_____

My Body and Brain Both Need a Break!

The brain is not designed for continuous input. It needs time for reflection, consolidation and integration. Sometimes the best results happen away from the formal learning, as an insight or an inspiration. Here are a few activities that give the brain a real break.

Suggestions

✔ **Writing your name with body parts.** Students stand up and "write" their first name with their elbow, their middle name with their other elbow, their last name with their hip, their best friend's name with their other hip and their mom or dad's name with their head.

✔ **Stretching.** The whole group stands up and stretches as a slow movement, fast fun, or as aerobics. All can be done to music (student's choice). It's best when it can be lead by a student, a rotating group leader or done to a theme. Can be done as a large group or in teams or groups of four or five.

✔ **Somebody's body.** Everyone stand up. Pair up with a partner. All pairs get 3 minutes to use some part of the body to measure something in the room. The goal is to invent the most bizarre or fun measuring. At the end of 5 minutes, the pairs report to the group their results: ("This cabinet is 210 knuckles long.").

✔ **Opposites attract.** All stand up. Pick a partner. One finds or touches an object in the room, the other has to find either a "go-with" (a similar item) or an opposite. The goal is to locate at least five pairs in one minute.

I tried which ideas today? What were the results?
What will I do differently next time?

_____

_____

_____

For Better Learning, Replace Rewards & Bribes

A reward is any consequence that is predictable and has market value to the learner. "Do this and you get that." Often used on the so-called "under-motivated" and "low achievers," rewards create unwanted side-effects including reduced intrinsic motivation and the "glass ceiling" on achievement. They encourage a predictable behavior, but in the long term the joy of learning is killed.

The brain is naturally motivated; it's a survival instinct to learn. The more we use tokens, bribes, coupons and rewards, the more the intrinsic motivation is conditioned out of the system and ruined. The old model was a demand-based behaviorist one; decide on the behavior you want and reward it. But, in the long run, rewards will reduce intrinsic motivation, impair higher-order thinking skills, reduce contextual memory and eliminate the love of learning. You can get your students to learn naturally, without bribes and without coercion. It's simple, and it works far better than the controlling, manipulative brain-antagonistic approach.

Suggestions

✔ Students create their own rewards for learning. Eliminate all bribes and rewards with your learners. Phase out any existing ones over time. Tell your learners why.

✔ Role-model the joy and love of learning so that it becomes learning for its own sake, not done for an extrinsic reward.

✔ Allow learners more choice and control in learning. This increases their intrinsic motivation.

✔ Increase the quantity and quality of feedback. This gives them the reinforcement needed without the rewards.

✔ Create more celebration and acknowledgment. This can help embed the value on a deeper level.

**I tried which ideas today? What were the results?
What will I do differently next time?**

_____

_____

_____

Discipline Strategies That Really Make Sense

Yes, there are specific, practical things that you can do to reduce the likelihood of discipline problems occuring and there are specific things you can do to successfully deal with them once they do occur. These strategies are based on several important concepts. First, our spatial memory links each experience with a location. Therefore, criticism, embarrassments and putdowns will be associated with you or your classroom. Avoid them. Second, all brain-body behaviors are state dependent. Keep learners in a good state for learning. Change their state if it happens to be a poor one for learning.

Suggestions

✔ Keep positive relationships, emotions, challenge and novelty in the learning. This will keep learners focused.

✔ Change activities when behavior is inappropriate. Whatever you're doing, change. Use a different form of the seven multiple intelligences, change your tone of voice, or your location in the room, change activities, whisper or take a stretch break.

✔ Manage the learner's "state," *not* the specific behaviors.

✔ Use a corner or hot spot for heavy discipline. Never be "heavy" from the front of the room; you'll contaminate that area with bad feelings. Go to your designated spot and use the same warning and gesture.

✔ Plant seeds for better behavior with specific storytelling and metaphors about the power of silence or restraint.

I tried which ideas today? What were the results?
What will I do differently next time?

_____

_____

_____

The Chemistry of Choice

We know that the brain acts differently when choice is offered. Choice changes the chemistry of the brain. How? When learners get to choose a task, the resources, or the parameters for accomplishment, their stress is lower. They feel more positive about the task and look forward to participating and hopefully, succeeding at it. This, in turn, triggers the release of our own "optimal thinking" brain chemicals. These endorphins consist of two chemicals, each a chain of five amino acids. The critical neurotransmitters involved in feeling confident appear to be dopamine and serotonin. A lack of choice changes the body's chemistry and that affects the attitude.

On the other hand, when we feel hopeless, lacking choices or depressed, the reaction is chemical, too. The brain produces norepinephrine, a neurotransmitter which has a strong inhibitory effect. In this brain state, morale is low, learning efficiency is poor and motivation is weak. Which comes first, the chemical changes or the outward states? It's probably both, depending on the circumstances.

Suggestions

✔ Instead of always using directive, controlling words, intersperse them with occasional softeners. Use expressions that offer choice, "You might like to..." or, "You may find..." or, "Others have found...."

✔ Allow your learners to continually make appropriate choices in their learning. They may select from a menu of topics or choose their own. The amount of choice offered should vary and be age-appropriate. Too much choice and learners will only do things they are familiar with. Too little, and they'll never get to develop a passion for learning.

✔ Learners may also create or have say-so in the criteria for assessment.

I tried which ideas today? What were the results?
What will I do differently next time?

_____

_____

_____

Hollywood Here I Come...Role-Play, Part II

There are so many versions of role-play, we might as well tap into a few more. They involve the kinesthetic, spatial, verbal linguistic part of us, they engage emotions and build problem-solving skills.

Suggestions

✔ **Expert Interviews.** Use for topic review. Half the audience becomes an expert in the topic you're teaching and half becomes the famous reporters doing the interviewing. Give students ten minutes to prepare. The reporters use the time to come up with key questions, the experts get into character and review their notes. Give about 5 minutes for the interviews. Switch partners. Make it dramatic with music or costumes. Experts & reporters then debrief the experience with each other.

✔ **Retro Party.** Great for when you need students to get into a historical "mood" for English, History, Science or any other subject. First, let students pair up and discuss how things might be different in that era: dress, posture, subjects, language, manners, etc. Next, all stand up, close eyes, and turn the clock back 20, 30, 50, 100 or 500 years to the era you're studying. Discuss topics that you might have discussed during that era. What objects would or wouldn't be in the room? Debrief.

✔ **The World's a Stage.** Pause in your lecture. Have students stand up, and find 3-5 others to form small groups. The goal of the group is to turn the last hour of lecture, learning or discussion into a 1-3 minute act (a role play). For example, they could become a giant solar system, complete with the sun, planets, moon, debris and comets. Or, they might role-play a discipline policy you just mentioned. They might act out a customer service skill or discuss the merits of a book used.

I tried which ideas today? What were the results?
What will I do differently next time?

_____

_____

_____

Reduce Common Forms of Perceived Threat

Our brain is strongly impacted by the four enemies of learning: threat, excess stress, anxiety and induced learner helplessness. Each of those causes the brain to "minimize," meaning you get less usage of the whole brain, and more engagement of the stored reactive behaviors. This reduces higher-order thinking skills, lessens creativity and diminishes memory. Threats can be as simple as "I'll just stand here and wait until you quiet down!" Anxiety can be as simple as the learner's inability to see and hear directions. It could be a bully in the hallway or a language barrier. Induced learner helplessness can be caused by nearly anything including: no pencil, no books, or a lack of time or resources to complete the assignment.

Suggestions

✔ Arrange no surprises in academics, like pop quizzes. Reassure the learners of the likelihood of their success.
✔ Make a "mistakes OK" climate for learning.
✔ Avoid "playground" or "street" discipline tactics which intimidate.
✔ Allow learners time to de-stress upon arrival in class through stretching, discussion, music, journaling or reflection.
✔ Never promise or threaten learners with having to stay after.

I tried which ideas today? What were the results?
What will I do differently next time?

_____

_____

_____

Secrets to Increase By-Product Learning

The brain is designed to learn. But the brain is poorly designed for traditional, formal instruction. So how do you deal with the paradox? A useful strategy is called by-product learning. This means you can make what is learned a fringe benefit, or an indirect result of the process. Games can boost recall for content and also, as a by-product, build friendships.

This reduces the didactic, heavy-handed relationship and encourages more of the "real-life" learning. So, in order to get to the goal, they do the learning, as an aside. In a five year-old's class, cooperative groups help complete a project, but they also build collaborative skills. In an adolescent math class, the students learn how to buy and remodel an imaginary house, and in the process, learn negotiation and research skills, math percentages, money and banking.

Suggestions

✔ Find out the kinds of activities that your learners like and integrate your key concepts into them.
✔ Use outdoor games to learn teamwork, self-confidence & trust.
✔ Create larger projects to learn multi-disciplinary concepts that require utilizing multiple resources and gaining new skills.
✔ Use cooperative learning to boost sharing, increase knowledge, and build meaning.
✔ Watch videos and television, discuss, and learn how to learn from them. Ask learners to write & draw conclusions from real life.

I tried which ideas today? What were the results?
What will I do differently next time?

_____

_____

_____

Learning with the Left AND Right Brain

The old model was that the left brain is for logic, order and reason. The right brain was for creativity, emotions and music. But we now know better. Both sides of the brain are involved in nearly every activity. You can use your left brain to be creative, as the work of DeBono taught us with lateral thinking. Surprisingly, musicians process music more in their left hemisphere than non-musicians. Should we try to appeal to both sides of the brain? Neuroscientists say that we use both sides of the brain for nearly every activity–it's simply a matter of relative specialization. Let's explore ways to appeal to both sides of the brain.

Suggestions

✔ Present a whole-unit, "big picture" globalization to start. Do this verbally (previews) and visually (video, organizers).
✔ After a global overview, provide a road map, a list, a sequence of steps for all learners.
✔ Keep posters and peripherals of the whole unit up on the walls so that the learners have a global map of the material. Use music, drama and physical movement.
✔ For important material, always let students know what's coming up next. There's always room for spontaneity.
✔ At the opening, throughout the lesson and closing, encourage learners to map out their understanding on paper.

I tried which ideas today? What were the results?
What will I do differently next time?

_____

_____

_____

Grow Out, Not Fill Up

The old way was to plan the content (i.e., "What do I want to do today to fill their brain?"). But that way was backwards (or upside down). The brain-based way is simple; it's planning for learning by adding outward to expand existing knowledge. You can extend natural knowledge or re-frame knowledge or change the context of the application. This approach is more student-centered, customer-based, learner-compatible and user-friendly.

Learners can't know your experience base, the details, the emotions, the depth and meaning you have. So the only place for them to start learning is from what they *already* know. Change the model from "fill up" their brains, to "grow out" their brains. The best lesson planning might include:

Suggestions

- ✔ **Preparation.** Use pre-exposure tools, create immersion environments, (students) do goal setting, give brain "wake-ups" like cross-laterals or relax-stretching. Have strong, positive expectations.
- ✔ **Globalization.** Start with what the learners know first. Discover and build outward. Context, overview, the classic "big picture" all are critical up-front strategies. Use with concrete experiences first!
- ✔ **Initiation.** Immersion in the topic: Flood with content! Try problem-solving, excursions, field trips, interviews or hands-on learning.
- ✔ **Elaboration.** Think, write, ask or design questions, go into data bases, restate questions, write a test, hold peer discussions, and create mind-maps.
- ✔ **Incubation.** Unguided reflection, "down time," a day off, a recess, journal writing time, relaxation time or simply a change of subjects.
- ✔ **Verification.** Students demonstrate what they know through self-tests or assessments.
- ✔ **Celebration.** Peer reinforcement, hi-fives, cheers, and acknowledgment.

I tried which ideas today? What were the results?
What will I do differently next time?

_____

_____

_____

Learning is Often Messy

That means multi-path learning with simultaneous inputs. We process sounds, touch, sights, smells and tastes, all at the same time. A museum, street walk, foreign country, a concert, guest speakers, a circus, festival, sporting event, fair or any new experience is terrific for growing dendrites, (the brain's cell connectors) for more associations and learning. Any lesson plan with a linear, lockstep, sequential single input approach may induce learning, but will likely be very unstimulating. Accordingly, presenters who use single modality teaching styles will most likely bore and frustrate their students.

Suggestions

✔ Offer learning centers, with multiple options. Take students to other sites for learning on campus.

✔ Increase audiovisual components, use multi-media presentations, use many different learning styles.

✔ Get students outside, take them to other locations or on field trips. Use all seven of the multiple intelligences.

✔ Raise your tolerance for discussion noise while you add more partner, group and teamwork.

✔ Split class into two classes, students teach with partners or teams on one side, you on the other. Get students more involved in the learning process.

I tried which ideas today? What were the results?
What will I *do* differently next time?

_____

_____

_____

4 Ways to Trigger Learning

First of all, much of what is important to the brain, cannot be easily measured with today's assessments. So, how do you know learning is going on? That's a tough question, even for today's neuroscientists. We have a good understanding of learning at the cellular level, but in the classroom things are far more complex. Is learning a behavior change? Is learning a change of opinion? Could learning be a feeling? Does only "at school" learning count? Can you be a poor test-taker, and still be considered smart? How much should "street-smart" skills count? The answers are tough. To trigger genuine learning, here are five powerful strategies.

Suggestions

✔ Demonstrate or discuss their mental models, "How did you go about figuring out that problem" Or, "How do you think we get our weather?" Ask students to explain, discuss, build and demonstrate models of what they know not just academically, but also intellectually and psychologically, and how they know it.

✔ Build their personal bias of that material. Being passionate about what you teach can help them learn to like it, too. Ask them to do a before and after rating ("how do I feel about this subject?") on a scale of 1-10.

✔ Teach the interdisciplinary relationships; how you can use math in geology, or what health science has to do with history. Ask students to demonstrate how this relates to other disciplines and topics. Ask students to demonstrate how the learning affects them or what it has to do with their neighborhood, community or world.

✔ Hook in the areas of personal relevance to them by starting with personal examples of your own before beginning academic ones.

**I tried which ideas today? What were the results?
What will I do differently next time?**

_____

_____

_____

Brain-Compatible Learning Avoids Labeling

In a brain-based approach, it makes no sense to call some learners a "high group" or others a "low group." Here are seven reasons why: 1) labeling a learner contributes to a self-fulfilling prophecy, 2) their strongest abilities may be in a multiple intelligence other than what you are offering or using for testing, 3) the label implies that the learner is somehow deficient or damaged goods, when in fact, they bring years of life experience to learning, 4) other presenters, in the past, may have been unskilled in bringing out the best in that learner, 5) our models of assessment are insufficient to measure all ranges of success, 6) the learner may be normal, but a couple of years behind the others in normal brain development. Variations are *typical.* 7) many of the greatest contributors to our society were labeled as "average" or "slow learners" in school, reminding us that we are still very poor at predicting greatness.

Suggestions

✔ Avoid ability grouping.
✔ Use more student-referenced mastery learning.
✔ Provide learning centers based on different intelligences.
✔ Avoid references to "fast, gifted, talented" or "slow" learners.
✔ Use the learner's background as a source of new learning (their ability to play basketball can be the basis for math (learning stats etc.), their desire to get rich may be a basis for learning economics).

I tried which ideas today? What were the results?
What will I *do* differently next time?

_____

_____

_____

Avoid Triggering Helpless Learning States

Under conditions of "induced learner helplessness" your learners will feel overwhelmed, anxious or resigned. Typically they will sit back and act helpless even with sufficient resources. There are two events usually: the original traumatic event and the secondary triggered event.

The original event usually involves intense threat and stress in the face of uncontrollable circumstances by the student. For example, being asked to read in front of classmates when you can't read very well, or a verbal threat such as, "One more time and you'll have to stay after!" The secondary event need not be as intense as the original.

Once a learner is immobilized with an initial threat, it takes time to desensitize them back to making positive, controlled learning choices. Lab experiments suggest it can take up to 30-50 trials with positive reinforcement to get a subject with induced helplessness to choose a better path. Teachers who give up on students after 3-5 attempts may erroneously label them as unmotivated. To break the cycle of learned helplessness, it takes repetition.

Suggestions

✔ Learn what level your learners are at: ask for a show of hands, use a written survey, observe students at work, ask others, find out background or history of the students.
✔ Make sure that students know what resources they have and do not have, before beginning a task.
✔ Allow partner or team collaboration on projects and assignments at least half the time. It boosts support.
✔ Get more feedback from the learners to find out what they know or don't know before continuing.
✔ Repeat directions slowly, if possible, give them both auditorily and visually.

I tried which ideas today? What were the results?
What will I do differently next time?

_____

_____

_____

Welcome to Center Stage!

The brain stores memories in our body, and our mind and locates them in space. We stimulate those stored memories through both content cues and context cues. The more the drama or role-play mimics the real-life physiological states needed, the more the memory can be retrieved when needed later. Several positive things happen when your learners engage in role-play.

First, they are more likely to participate. Second, the type of roles often engage emotions, which can stimulate long term memory. The memory of the activity would be stored in the body as much as the mind. Lastly, learners are more likely to draw meaning from the activity. Meaning comes from emotions and larger patterns of understanding, both of which are supplied by these activities.

Suggestions

✔ Make sure learners get choice in the process of creating the role-plays or game shows.

✔ Design these activities so that they are as close to the real thing in terms of skills, ideas and information.

✔ Make sure that they have a reason to do these, so that learners are excited and purposeful about doing them.

✔ Insure that the competition is win-win so that everyone feels safe and willing to do it again sometime.

✔ Set it up so that emotions are engaged. Use teams, music, deadlines, and sound effects. Without them, it is just another form of busy work.

I tried which ideas today? What were the results?
What will I do differently next time?

_____

_____

_____

Bring Simon (Simone) Back From the Grave!

Dozens of childhood games are brilliant for learning, listening and building skills. Why? They can combine fun with learning! Sometimes, we have bad memories of a game from years ago because of the way the game was set up and run, not the game itself. For example, when I play "Simon Says" with my audiences, there are no losers. No one is embarrassed or humiliated. No one has to sit down and be "out of the game." If you make a mistake, just keep playing! You know when you make a mistake; there's no need to add salt to the wound. Now, take the game of Simon and try out as many variations as you can.

Suggestions

✔ **Simon Says.** All stand and do only what Simon (you) says to do. Give instructions to follow, some of them prefaced with "Simon says," and others not. Go at a moderate pace. If they make a mistake, keep playing. Always make it a win for all, so one's ever out of the game.

✔ **Variations.** You can use it as: 1) A listening game, for following instructions, 2) A "get to know you" game, pointing to, saying or facing a person you call out, 3) A geography game... "Simon Says point to the direction of Alaska or point to Australia," 4) A math game... "Simon says use your body to give me the answer to 5 plus 6," 5) Language learning... "Simon says, point to 'su boca' or 'su mano,' 6) A science game..."Simon says, point to something in this room made of steel... point to something made of glass... made of plastic... that's over twenty years old... that would't have existed 50 years ago..."

I tried which ideas today? What were the results?
What will I do differently next time?

_____

_____

_____

Magic Learning Formula

The brain is biologically designed to do some things that you can take advantage of in the classroom. First, we all seek the stimulation that comes from novelty. The use of novelty keeps attention and interest. A new idea, a new food, a new outfit can all be exciting. The flip side is that we seek the non-threatening, safety and security of familiarity. Always balance novelty with predictability.

In the classroom, the use of repetitive, purposeful rituals keeps the learners feeling safe and familiar. The final, third element is the process: a challenge. Too much challenge and we feel overwhelmed. Too little challenge evokes inertia. Just the right amount, where the degree of task difficulty matches the learner's skill level, and the learner now feels safe to explore and be challenged by a task which is neither too hard or too easy. That's the essence of natural, intrinsic motivation.

Suggestions

✔ Allow the learners a greater part in the teaching process. Let them plan and teach a mini-lesson. That creates novelty and challenge.

✔ Initiate productive and purposeful classroom rituals. Examples include call-backs, start-ups, and closing. Others include stretch breaks, distraction breaks, acknowledgments and celebrations.

✔ Vary the resources available to create the optimal challenge. To make tasks harder, make them more complex, add a public presentation to it, or set higher standards. To make them easier, give more time, provide teammates or partners, or provide key information.

I tried which ideas today? What were the results?
What will I do differently next time?

_____

_____

_____

Stimulating Input, Not Just Output

Surprisingly, the brain grows by novel input, not by what the students express. Novel input is what makes the brain reorganize, reallocate nerve cells to other areas and stimulate better neuronal connections. As a musician listens to new notes, bars and chords, parts of the auditory cortex are reassigning cells in the brain to be better at it for the next time. As an athlete tries out a new behavior, the brain grows new branching to be able to perform the maneuver. In classroom learning, novel and challenging problem-solving is one way to "grow" the brain. Another way is through purposeful multi-sensory stimulation.

Suggestions

✔ Allow students to do rocking, spinning and bouncing exercises. These include, but are not limited to, swings, merry-go-rounds and jump rope. These stimulate the vestibular (inner ear).

✔ Expose students to new types of music. Experiment with world music, jazz, drumming, Mozart and Indian music.

✔ Ask students to try out new forms of stretching, create new versions of handshakes, novel celebration rituals or greetings.

✔ Have students trace strange or foreign objects.

✔ Ask students to talk about what they are thinking while they are working on a project, solving a problem or simply observing. Do this into a tape recorder, or have another student serve as a journal-maker. They might be saying, "I am now holding my pencil at a 45 degree angle. I'm pressing lightly as I begin the first word of my essay...."

I tried which ideas today? What were the results?
What will I do differently next time?

_____

_____

_____

New Importance in Beginnings and Endings

The brain responds to information first in a survival orientation. We react the most to beginnings, endings, and new circumstances. If adaptive, it certainly is a useful instinct: a dangerous roar and we run, the roar disappears and we relax. In the classroom, learners imprint most actively to your starts and finishes, openings and closing. Change creates an attentional bias and signals the possibility of something important coming up. You get windows of opportunity for special attention when you start and when you end, so be sure to take advantage of the brain's natural receptiveness.

Suggestions

✔ Try this one: Make sure your class openings provide critical learning. You might summarize key points in the first 30 seconds. Or, you might do a quick call-response review on the previous day's contents.

✔ Devise rituals to deal with unwanted interruptions. Make it fun to deal with distractions. After all, where the attention goes, the energy goes. Might as well "ride the horse in the direction it's going!" Teach students to turn in the direction of the walk-in guest and say all at once, "Welcome to third grade with Mrs. Peterson." This lets everyone "get it out" all at once.

✔ Provide frequent breaks to create more beginnings and endings. Do quick reviews before and after them.

✔ Break attention patterns with frequent novelty and challenge. For example, ask students to stand up and give a 3 minute mini-lecture.

✔ Make sure that your openings and class endings have a strong emotional appeal. Do this with action, music, sharing or celebration.

I tried which ideas today? What were the results?
What will I *do* differently next time?

_____

_____

_____

1...2...3...Switch Jobs

Need a break from your job? Maybe it would be great for your audience, too. A great memory strategy, as well as an enriching experience for the learners, is a guest speaker. But where do you get them? You would be surprised how easy it is.

As a teacher, you might make it a class project for one week. The students could build a class "yellow page" of all the things the students are good at, what their parents are good at, and what others in the community may be good at. You may have a great source of guest speakers right at your fingertips.

As a trainer, You'd be surprised how easy it is to find guest speakers. In the area you work in, there may be a directory of speakers, or at least professionals. For example, in neuroscience, there's a membership directory of the 25,000 members. I use it as a way to find speakers. While this is more the exception than the rule, I found a world-famous Nobel-prize laureate who was willing to speak to a group I had for free. That's right, free. The moral of the story: there's no harm in asking.

Suggestions

✔ Use the real yellow pages as a source of speakers.
✔ Students create a classroom directory of services (student Yellow Pages). Then add the skills, knowledge or experiences your students have (like telling jokes, fixing things, computers, pets, music, etc.).
✔ Create a school or business yellow pages from all the other trainers, teachers or staff (including custodial) who have expertise.
✔ Scan the newspapers for local authors who might be willing to come speak for a few minutes.

I tried which ideas today? What were the results?
What will I do differently next time?

_____

_____

_____

Cycles of Learning

Are your learners more right or left brained? They are probably both. In fact, the brain has a natural fluctuation from one hemisphere to another over the course of a day, usually on 90 minute cycles. At the top of the up-down cycle, you'll be more right-brained and at the top of the next cycle, you'll be more left-brained. You've experienced this yourself: You're working hard at something very linear, sequential and ZAP! Within seconds, you go brain dead and need to take a break. That same shift happens to your learners.

They can get either "left-brain stuck" or "right-brain stuck." The left side stuck is, "I've tried over and over to solve this problem, every path has been a dead end." The "right side stuck" is more overwhelming: "I'm lost–this stuff is too much." Be sure to have a "toolbox" of strategies to awaken the brain and activate both sides. In the long term, the cycles are fairly permanent. But four things can affect those highs and lows short-term; exercise, nutrition, emotions and cross laterals.

Suggestions

✔ Have more understanding and acceptance about your learner's normal cycles. They include highs and lows every 90 minutes, alternating hemispheric dominance. When students get stuck, don't label them.

✔ Talk to them about how the brain works so they understand enough to be empowered in their learning. Give them examples and information about it. Give them a choice so that they can do more low-key activities at the low parts of their cycle.

✔ Allow learners more mobility in the classroom during specific times. Provide errands they can do, a jump rope, or just let them stand or walk around.

✔ Learn cross-lateral activities: marching in place while patting opposite knees, patting yourself on the opposite side of the back and touching opposite elbows.

I tried which ideas today? What were the results?
What will I do differently next time?

_____

_____

_____

Use Multiple Strategies for Better Recall

Research suggests that our memories are not stored in any picture form. We simply recreate them on the spot, each time we want to recall something. There's no memory center in our brain, but we recall things with an impromptu composition by all the triggered experiences. This means our existing memories will change; they'll be altered by our experiences, values, beliefs and biases.

The greater the variety of learning input, the more accurate the recall. Sights, smells, sounds, and touch all create (as a whole) more complex and rich memories than a workbook or a multi-media CD. Your learners, even under the best of conditions, need continual opportunities to share, discuss, map, journal, teach and reorganize the learning. That not only keeps it fresh, but it encourages deeper meaning.

Suggestions

✔ Immediately after learning, have students discuss, draw or act out the material.

✔ The following day, ask students to mind map the material, then peer teach what they have mapped.

✔ Weekly, ask students to put the material into perspective though discussions or adding to larger maps or projects.

✔ Encourage and organize longer projects that require lengthy understanding of the material instead of quick, short out-of-context facts.

✔ Ask students to do end of course summaries, build models, produce videos, do interviews, draw larger maps or teach the class, to reinforce learning.

I tried which ideas today? What were the results?
What will I do differently next time?

_____

_____

_____

Hydration Boosts Student Learning

There's been research lately on the role of hydration in the learning process. At first, only athletes were thought to suffer impaired performance when the body was low on fluids. But now, some researchers believe that the thinking, problem-solving and creative processes are slowed, too. The body and the brain is 70% water. But can drinking water affect us that much? New evidence suggests that possibility.

Your brain runs on electrochemical reactions. The cells (neurons) have membranes which maintain a specific polarity. These membranes maintain both a positive and negative charge, ranging from -70mv to +70 mv. But a change of only 30 millivolts can mean death. A change in the amount of water in the body can affect the charge. Dehydration can happen even with coffee, or tea (diuretics which are used up too fast through urination) or soft drinks or juice (which uses up water because it treats it as food and binds with sugar to draw it away from the brain).

Suggestions

✔ Role model drinking water during your class.
✔ Encourage students to drink water right before class.
✔ Talk to your students about the role of hydration and the brain.
✔ Allow students to bring clear liquids in "sport bottles."
✔ During class, allow students to leave to get a drink.

I tried which ideas today? What were the results?
What will I do differently next time?

_____

_____

_____

Build Brain Maps and New Learning Patterns

Does our brain think sequentially or in multi-directional maps? Our thinking processes are both linear and random. As we think, learn and grow, our brain makes individual connections from one cell to another through dendritic branching. But each cell can also connect with dozens, hundreds or even thousands of other cells simultaneously in a three dimensional, rain forest, jungle matrix. Inside our brain, the process of learning is enriched by making more associations, on more levels, to more things, people and experiences.

Suggestions

✔ Before beginning, "jump-start" the topic by reviewing what was learned in the past or by making new associations in a fun, quick game.

✔ Ask the learners to create a huge conceptual model or map of what they already know on the topic before starting.

✔ Teach your students graphic organizers, mapping and mindscapes.

✔ Provide global overviews before beginning and at the end of a unit.

✔ At the end of a unit, ask students to create large concept maps to pull together all their learning on a topic in a colorful, pictorial way.

I tried which ideas today? What were the results?
What will I do differently next time?

_____

_____

_____

Why Use Aromas in Learning?

Scientists have been studying the impact of aromas on the brain for years. Smells affect several areas of the brain including the limbic area, which is responsible for attention. You've already noticed that the smell of freshly baked bread, cookies or popcorn raises attention and awareness levels dramatically. Why? the sense of smell is processed differently than any other sense and it gets a quicker, uninterrupted and unfiltered access to the brain. This means that you'll actually have reactions to the aroma before you have any conscious awareness that you've inhaled them. But what specific aromas are useful for learning?

Suggestions

✔ Occasionally use new aromas to trigger the brain's attention.
✔ Encourage students to bring in aromatic items.
✔ Fresh lemon, cinnamon or peppermint oils are exceptional.
✔ Fresh, aromatic flowers can be effective.
✔ Use fans, leaves, air fresheners, ionizers and fruit.
✔ Be respectful of those with allergies.

I tried which ideas today? What were the results?
What will I do differently next time?

_____

_____

_____

Let the Brain Nibble at New Ideas

Have you ever tried to explain a powerful, mind-boggling new concept to someone? They just don't get it at first. Why? Because they have no prior information or experience to relate it to. The brain's dendrites need to connect with other dendrites through synaptic connections. The more associations, the better the understanding. A strong neural network of these connections helps us create mental models.

Our understanding of a concept is based in part on the development of past models. But a new paradigm lacks the existing networks to establish understanding. You can understand parts of a new paradigm, but not the whole model, all at once.

To help your learners understand and absorb big concepts, use the "cookie crumb" idea. Leave a trail of "idea crumbs" along the path to learning. Start before you get to a topic and continue even after you've long since finished a topic.

Suggestions

✔ Use pre-exposure of the material to plant seeds of learning far in advance.
✔ Use discovery mapping to help uncover what learners *already* know before starting a new topic.
✔ Show a video before starting a topic to connect it to existing knowledge.
✔ Do word association games to trigger old and new thoughts. Have discussions on related themes.
✔ Give the learners a concrete experience of the concept as early into the learn ing as possible.

I tried which ideas today? What were the results?
What will I do differently next time?

_____

_____

_____

Hollywood, You've Arrived! Role-Play, Part III

Role-play is so important to learning that I thought I'd share some more great ideas for the classroom. Remember to add applause and celebration!

Suggestions

✔ **Get to know me charades.** Stand, pick a partner, tell that partner 3 things about yourself using no words, only charades. They tell you 3 things... Or, they could demonstrate 3 things about your school, your company, an idea...?

✔ **Instant replay.** Stand and pick partners. One acts it out, the other replays it. Add subject matter content to make it more valuable. You might add time restraints and sounds, then words.

✔ **City Night Sounds.** One team at a time picks a group of sounds that might be heard in any big city. On stage, they begin to make their sounds, then you add other teams, until you have the sound of a full city. Then a round of applause for all. Does it have to be "City Night?" No, you can also do a school, a conference or a jungle, a business, etc.

I tried which ideas today? What were the results?
What will I do differently next time?

_____

_____

_____

Eat Better to Boost Learning

How much do eating habits affect learning? A great deal. Foods are a source of carbohydrates and sugar for energy. They are the source of protein for amino acids. They have the ingredients to either release or block the neurotransmitters that make us alert or sleepy. They even help us remember things. The time of day and order in which you eat, makes as much difference as the particular foods you select. In total, effects on the amount of learning range from as little as 10% to as much as 65% in a typical student. Some recommendations are listed below.

Suggestions

✔ Eat more proteins and fruits early in the day, starches and meats later.

✔ Eat protein with sugars to reduce the "sugar effect."

✔ Foods that are best for the brain include: eggs, wheat germ, salmon, unsaturated fats, brazil nuts, dark green leafy vegetables, apples, bananas and lean meats.

✔ Drink plenty of water between meals, little with a meal.

✔ The brain runs best on a more consistant "nibbling diet."

✔ Get the word out to parents at open house about nutrition.

✔ Talk to your kids about it and role-model good habits

I tried which ideas today? What were the results?
What will I do differently next time?

_____

_____

_____

Better Learning with Unguided Discussions

Which is better, presenter-directed discussions or open, unguided student discussions? It depends on the topic. If the topic is academic, the younger ones (up to ages ten) do better with presenter-directed. Older students do better without presenter direction. Studies suggest that the most likely way to get learner-motivated change is to allow students unguided discussion time on the topic. The more learners feel controlled, directed and manipulated, the less likely they are to change their behavior.

Suggestions

✔ Within a topic, have the learners generate discussion questions. Ask the learners to also generate test questions.

✔ Before beginning a topic, ask learners what they'd like to learn.

✔ Find out what learners already know about a topic. Use discussion groups, mind maps, etc.

✔ Give learners 5-20% of total class time for discussion. Could be with partners or teams.

✔ De-brief discussion time to understand the process better. Could be as a group or even in journal writing.

I tried which ideas today? What were the results?
What will I do differently next time?

_____

_____

_____

Get Real Physical and Go to War

Many learners can hear something over and over and not get it. Sometimes they just need to learn it kinesthetically. One of my favorite ways to do that is with a tug-of-war. This activity can either be brilliantly designed for fun or a real bust if it's done poorly. Here are some suggestions to make it work brilliantly.

Suggestions

✔ **Supplies needed.** An old braided fiber rope can cause rope burns. The newer super-fine nylon ones are best. Make sure participants are wearing the right clothing. Make sure that you have a large, safe place to hold this activity. To set up the activity, everyone gets a partner and picks a topic from the list that all have been learning. Each person has their own topic and their goal is to convince their partner in an argument why their topic is more important (or will be on the test, or is the key topic, etc.).

✔ **Go to War.** After a one minute, stand-up, face-to-face debate, you say it has to be settled physically. Go outside to a giant tug of war, with all partners on opposite sides. Keep in reserve any players who are undecided about their topic. They'll be off to the side for the moment. Once the game gets started, you can use them to balance the teams better. Anyone can switch sides if they change their mind on their topic. When done have a celebration for everyone.

I tried which ideas today? What were the results?
What will I do differently next time?

_____

_____

_____

Enriched Environments Can Boost Learning

Is the human brain structurally "set" for life or is it malleable? Astonishing research found that the brain not only can be structurally modified by enriching experiences, but that the changes can occur within as little as four days! The brain is designed to respond to stimuli by physically growing new, larger and more extensive dendritic branching. It also releases more enzymes, forms more glial cells (a form of brain "lubricant"), grows larger synapses (the connectors between cells) and gets heavier. Furthermore, this growth can happen *at any age* as long as the brain is stimulated properly.

Suggestions

✔ Provide frequent new learning experiences. Student teams can alternate novel presentations.

✔ Challenge and novelty are particularly valuable. Provide guest speakers, new locations and use props.

✔ Increase the frequency of feedback to your learners. Help them get feedback at least every 30 minutes or less.

✔ Arrange for greater positive social interaction. It could be pair and share or group work.

✔ Make the physical environment more stimulating with colorful, interesting peripherals, hands-on materials, aromas, music, multi-sensory experiences and flexible seating.

I tried which ideas today? What were the results?
What will I do differently next time?

_____

_____

_____

Succeed with the SAT Method

There are seven styles of communicating, from one extreme to another. You can demand, threaten, tell, suggest, ask, imply and hope. It is usually inappropriate to demand or threaten. It is rarely effective to imply or hope. The brain responds most favorably to physiological states of relaxation, intent and alertness. Only the tonalities, volume and tempo of suggest, ask and tell (S-A-T) communicate to the student the best learning states.

Suggestions

✔ Suggest to your learners how capable they are, how easy they'll learn & how valuable they'll find the learning.
✔ Provide choice so that they feel in control of their own learning.
✔ Suggest they might want to explore the topic further on their own time, in other areas, in greater detail.
✔ Tell your learners to do things when you have less time and explain to the students that *how* they completed the task is important to you.
✔ Ask learners to do things that they might want to do anyway so that they get the feeling of choice.

I tried which ideas today? What were the results?
What will I do differently next time?

_____

_____

_____

Brain Activators for the Visual Cortex

What is good for the brain when it comes to visual enrichment? There are many activities. Many of the ones listed elsewhere in this book are useful, but here are a few that are specifically great for activating the visual area of the brain.

Suggestions

✔ **Changing environments.** It can be done by changing seats, locations within the room, a field trip, where you stand, changing the posters or room decorations, temperature, music, or many others.

✔ **Windows.** Some research says that having windows to look out of is good for the brain. You say your students get too distracted? Hmm...maybe they just need an "attention break" or more relevant choice or engagement.

✔ **Show-do** (e.g. Simon-Says). These simple games are explained elsewhere in greater detail.

✔ **Natural and incandescent lighting.** Many studies indicate these are good for learning. You say all you have is fluorescent? Can you change the bulbs? Can you do things in other locations? Can you go outside at times?

✔ **What's missing from this picture?** What's different? What has changed? You can do this with your students and they can do it with a partner. It could be from the front of the room or on your own person. Identification of nearly everything.

I tried which ideas today? What were the results?
What will I do differently next time?

_____

_____

_____

Give Learners Environmental Options

Should your learners be given fixed seating or not? In most cases, your learners will do better if offered variety and choice. Studies done on many different types of learners found that 20% overall, needed mobility to be at their best. These kinesthetic-external (tactile) learners may need to stand, move, sit on the floor or walk around at times. Some are visual learners who want to sit up front or near the best "show" in the room. Auditory learners usually prefer cooperative learning while others will want to sit alone. The side of the room affects learning, too. Learners in the presenter's left side will be taking in the information more dominantly in their right hemisphere and vice versa.

Suggestions

✔ You might change sides of the room from where you usually speak.
✔ Put learners in groups at least once a day.
✔ Alternate from individual learning to partnership learning often.
✔ Give students choice of how to learn for at least part of the class.
✔ Let learners create new environments often by re-arranging the seating.

I tried which ideas today? What were the results?
What will I do differently next time?

_____

_____

_____

How to Grab the Brain's Attention

The two biological mechanisms built into the human brain (relating to attention-getting) are both survival based.

First, changes (often referred to as contrast and novelty) get the brain's attention. The larger, quicker ones get the most attention. Slow changes (trends) are poorly detected by the brain.

Second, the other attention-getter is any emotionally laden information. We are riveted by scenes on television of tragedy, terror, exhilaration, starvation, celebration, suspense and sadness. Naturally, the newspapers, television and movies play up events such as a plane crash, a war, a homecoming, a dramatic sports match, a freeway police chase or a trapped baby. You can capitalize on this knowledge.

Suggestions

✔ Use suspenseful questions, moving personal examples and "idea teasers."
✔ Involve the students more in presentations since students are often a rich source of novelty.
✔ Use more props, costumes and voice changes. Let the students *wear* props.
✔ Use drama, music and role plays to emphasize ideas.
✔ Put more celebration in the learning process.

I tried which ideas today? What were the results?
What will I do differently next time?

_____

_____

_____

Why It's Good to Both Laugh and Learn

Is laughing good for learning? Many researchers think so. It seems that laughter increases the flow of the brain's neurotransmitters that are needed for alertness and memory. It also lowers the stress and improves functioning of the immune system. Laughter can provide a valuable change of "state" for students who may be stressed or anxious. Does this mean that the classroom should be a place for jokes? It's more useful to think of them as a productive break than a major part of learning.

Suggestions

✔ Avoid punishing learner-contributed humor if it's in good taste and fits within the time available in class.

✔ Use humor in your own presentations with stories or jokes.

✔ Bring in humorous video or audiotapes to play at needed moments.

✔ Have a ritual for daily or weekly "joke time" where students can share the latest jokes in small groups.

✔ Put up cartoons on overheads or post on the wall, but make sure that they are in good taste.

I tried which ideas today? What were the results?
What will I do differently next time?

_____

_____

_____

Activate Both Hemispheres With Cross Laterals

Students often get stuck in learning. A "left hemisphere stuck" is when a student says, "I've tried four different ways, and I still can't solve this problem." A "right hemisphere stuck" is when a student says, "I'm overwhelmed, I don't know what to do." Several studies suggest that specific, applied physical activity can change the physiological and mental "stuck" states. The secret is doing brief stand-up movements that cross arms or legs over (the body's center meridian) from one side of the body to another. These work by forcing the left and right hemisphere to interact vigorously with each other. That leads to better quality thinking and better quality learning.

Suggestions

✔ Stand and take a deep breath. Reach across the body and pat yourself on the back. Now switch hands and pat the other side of the back.

✔ Stand and reach behind your body and touch your opposite heel as you lift it. Alternate, switching to touch the opposite heel.

✔ Stand and touch or pat the opposite thigh. Alternate.

✔ Extend your hand straight in front, making a "thumbs up" sign. Now, move thumb upward towards the right and around in a sideways "8" or infinity sign. Cross the "X" of the 8 front and center. Do this 5-10 times, and switch hands.

✔ Stand and "swim" in place doing freestyle stroke with one arm and the backstroke with the other for 10 stokes. Switch and alternate directions.

I tried which ideas today? What were the results?
What will I do differently next time?

_____

_____

_____

Use the Mind-Body Library of Knowledge

Is learning just a mental process? Or can learning be stored in our bodies? Research indicates that we have different libraries of knowledge that are "state dependent." Whatever is learned in one particular state is most easily accessed again in that same particular state. Let's say you're in one room of your house and you think of a book that you want to get in another room. You start walking towards it, and halfway there, you suddenly realize you've forgotten what you were going to get! What do you do? You probably retraced your steps, going back to the room where you thought of the original idea. You stood in the same place (in the same state, most likely) and recalled the item.

Students who study for a test in a relaxed, low-key state will under-perform at test time if they feel the test is stressful. Students who study under higher stress will do better if the test is fairly stressful. In other words, we do best when the learned states match the recalling or performance states.

Suggestions

✔ Match the learning and testing states better. Or, create a third state–the rehearsal state. That way, what's learned can be more easily recalled.

✔ Teach under both low and moderate stress to help both kinds of test-takers.

✔ At test time, let students de-stress by standing for a stretch, drinking water, or doodling.

✔ Use the variety of assessment methods mentioned elsewhere in this book so that students are more able to show what they know.

✔ If you use written tests, make them more fun. Put cartoons on them, affirmations of success and test tips. For example, question 12 could be "Take in a slow deep breath, hold it for the count of three and exhale slowly," or "double check your answers!"

I tried which ideas today? What were the results?
What will I do differently next time?

_____

_____

_____

The Best Learning Environment

Several studies have demonstrated the power of natural lighting. Learners focused longer and performed better with full-spectrum florescent, incandescent bulbs, or natural lighting. The brain becomes dramatically inefficient when the air temperature is too warm. The best temperature for learning is 67-70 degrees. In fact, a rise of just 1-2 degrees in brain temperature is enough to impair learning (A heat stroke can occur with a 4 degree rise).

Suggestions

✔ Keep windows open, use natural lighting when possible. Get learners outside when possible. Otherwise, get the full-spectrum florescent or incandescent bulbs.
✔ Remind the learners to dress appropriately.
✔ Keep the room temperature slightly on the cool side.

I tried which ideas today? What were the results?
What will I do differently next time?

_____

_____

_____

Exercise and Activities Boost Learning

Several positive things happen with more active learning. First, there's more blood flow in the body which brings more oxygen to the brain. Second, it can trigger the release of the body's "good feeling" drug, endorphin or the "challenge" hormone, adrenaline. Studies show that these are excellent for the brain. In addition, the body is often activated into states of movement which make more enthusiasm and motivation likely. And finally, activities that are learned with the body are more likely to be recalled and applied at a later date. Mind-body movement gives the body more sensory clues to be able to re-address the learning in the future.

Suggestions

✔ Plan some kind of activity for most of your planned learning. These can be simple unit reviews using games of ball-toss or musical chairs.
✔ Include many stretch breaks at 10-20 minute intervals.
✔ Encourage learners to be active, play sports and exercise daily.
✔ Invite learners to stand and do simple deep breathing exercises.
✔ Get student input for activities like drama and role play.

I tried which ideas today? What were the results? What will I do differently next time?

_____

_____

_____

Use Eye Patterns to Affect Thinking

Researchers have discovered that where you move your eyes affects how you think. These generalizations hold true for nearly 90% of the population. Looking up activates the visual part of the brain. Looking to the upper left helps recall, and looking to the upper right helps construct. Looking to the left side activates auditory-internal, for recalling sounds. Looking to the right side allows you to construct sounds. Looking down and to the right allows you to experience feelings and it's down and to the left to create internal dialogue.

Suggestions

✔ Allow learners more space around themselves at test-time so they can let their eyes wander without being accused of cheating.
✔ Put peripherals up high for best stored recall.
✔ Stand to the learner's left to help them recall what you said.
✔ Use matching vocabulary when in conversation. If their eyes are up and searching, use visual predicates ("Look here..."). If their eyes are moving from side to side, use phrases with auditory predicates, "Listen, if this sounds good...." For those with downward, kinesthetic movements, use feeling words to talk. "How does this idea feel to you?"

I tried which ideas today? What were the results?
What will I do differently next time?

_____
_____
_____

Learn How Air Quality Can Boost Learning

Our brain is highly sensitive to environmental conditions. The atmosphere has an electrical charge to it. It can be neutral, negative or positive. Stuffy, confined, recirculated air is usually positively charged. The air is highly negatively charged around a waterfall, or when you step outside just after a fresh rain or get out of the shower. Highly negatively charged air increases brain serotonin, which is associated with lower stress and relaxed moods. Rats raised in a negatively ionized atmosphere grew a nearly 10% larger brain.

Suggestions

✔ Provide ample air circulation, preferably fresh air.
✔ Put fresh green plants in the room. The ones most recommended are dracaenas, spider plants and ficus.
✔ Purchase and use a negative ion generator. You may order one by calling (800) 382-IONS.
✔ Get learners outdoors when appropriate.

I tried which ideas today? What were the results?
What will I do differently next time?

_____

_____

_____

The Value of Chaos

Many times, a presenter strives to remove chaos from the classroom. And, obviously, there are times when that is useful. But the brain is not designed to work in an environment of constant equilibrium. In fact, some neuroscientists say that learning only occurs during impasses and emerges from confusion states. The real world offers a rich roller-coaster ride of emotions from high to low. A typical brain-antagonistic classroom is a constant effort by an unknowing presenter to keep everything at an even keel. Yet states of anticipation, excitement, uncertainty, challenge, suspense and release are the emotions that enhance attention, meaning and memory.

Suggestions

✔ Use more learner-generated role-plays, theater & drama.
✔ Allow for more open-ended discussions, take occasional tangents.
✔ Ask learners to make presentations so often that little preparation is necessary and the feeling is impromptu.
✔ Organize guest speakers with new activities.
✔ Get the students outside the classroom, either to other parts of the school or on field trips.

I tried which ideas today? What were the results?
What will I do differently next time?

_____

_____

_____

How Goal-Setting Boosts Performance

One strategy to maintain learner focus and concentration is goal-setting. Goals do several things. First, they narrow the attention span to the task at hand. Second, they can provide hope of reaching the goal; the anticipated pleasure. This often triggers the release of the body's "feel good" chemicals, the endorphins. But to get the most out of a goal-setting activity, there are some guidelines to follow.

Suggestions

✔ You might set some of the criteria, but the goals are set by the learner.
✔ The goals are specific, positive and reachable. Set high enough to be a real "win" but not so high as to discourage.
✔ The student generates their own WIIFM ("What's in it for me?"). Ask them to list all the benefits of reaching their goals. How would they feel, how would others feel, what would it do for them, etc.
✔ Students may change and re-direct their own goals as needed. The goals have to be reassessed and reevaluated or they become worthless.
✔ No presenter rewards are offered.

I tried which ideas today? What were the results?
What will I do differently next time?

_____
_____
_____

Making Unforgettable Memories Can Be Easy

One of the biggest problems with learners and presenters is called "contamination." That occurs when too many content items are learned in the same place. The brain lacks distinctive addresses for the ideas. If you sat in a college classroom and were lectured to for a semester, sitting in the same seat, with the same professor, for the same hour of time, after a while it would be hard to remember what was said. To your brain, the learning has all the same contextual location, so we say it's "contaminated."

The solution is to create as many separate "addresses" for the learning as we can. An address requires a specific location or specific circumstance. What were you doing July 19th, 1969? You probably don't remember. Do you remember where you were on July 20th, 1969? That was the day of the first moon landing. Naturally, you are also likely to recall birthdays, anniversary dates and unusual trips. In the classroom, the more distinctive the location or circumstances, the more likely your learners will remember it.

Suggestions

✔ Allow learners to change the physical location (seating) of their learning to prevent contamination.

✔ You can change which side of the room you stand (best to switch with new units or new twists on a subject).

✔ At test time, allow learners to sit where they want (as long as each learner's privacy is respected).

✔ Make props (hats, accessories, etc.) available to students. It creates a more distinct library for learning.

✔ Engage emotions to help mark out the learning. Use arguments, role-plays, debates, tug-of-war, journals, personal sharing, etc.

I tried which ideas today? What were the results?
What will I do differently next time?

_____

_____

_____

Encourage Faster Learning with Pre-Exposure

The brain is poorly designed to learn big new ideas, whole paradigm shifts, or new subject areas all at once. It is very good at "nibbling" at ideas, one bit of relevant material at a time. Every subject that we have learned well, we have learned over time, not all at once. But the reality of education is that we have very little time to bring out the learning. So what's the solution? Pre-exposure is a strategy that gives the learner small glimpses or experiences or sounds of the learning far in advance of the moment needed for success.

Television is continually giving you "sneak previews" of upcoming shows. They often "bait" you with enticing blurbs or unfinished plots to get you to tune in. Although their purpose is ratings, it also informs you. Give your learners continued pre-exposure of the content. It creates the mental "hooks" for further ideas and details to attach meaning to...almost like Velcro for the brain.

Suggestions

✔ Post up a graphic organizer, a mural or mind map on the wall 2-4 weeks in advance of that topic.

✔ Mention continual references to subjects, examples, topics and ideas that you'll get to in a few weeks.

✔ Show a video or have a guest speak on a topic well in advance.

✔ Ask learners to research one topic that also requires they get exposure to another.

✔ Use role-play and other activities that have similar themes, actions or structure to pre-expose students to the topic that they'll be learning later.

I tried which ideas today? What were the results?
What will I do differently next time?

_____

_____

_____

Learners Should Know that they Know

It's one thing for your learners to learn something; it happens almost automatically. But it's quite another thing to KNOW that you know it. This state of "knowing" is triggered by many learners automatically. But for many others, they simply don't know how they learn or how they know what they know. The secret is to provide for the learners three things: 1) review or reinforcement in their favorite modality (visual, auditory or kinesthetic) 2) Provide multiple options, so that they can review it several times, several ways 3) Make sure that the review lasts long enough for the learners to really know it. This is the state that you see in a learner when he or she just figures out how to solve a problem are when they sit back with that smug look that says, "I did it!"

Suggestions

✔ Give learners a chance to review learning in multiple modalities. They need to see reinforcement, hear it and touch it.

✔ Insure that the learners get a chance to reinforce their learning several times. For example, they can peer teach the material twice in a row, to a different person each time.

✔ Put celebration in the learning process. Learners can hear special music, get congratulated, get a certificate and feel the pride of achievement. (No rewards)

✔ Help learners know what they know through multiple types of review. One day, they mind-map it, another day, they build a model, another day, they answer questions, etc.

I tried which ideas today? What were the results?
What will I do differently next time?

_____

_____

_____

Appendix

References

Are there studies that suggest you can build a brighter brain with specific strategies, problem-solving and physical activity? Yes there are. While most of these references are from technical journals, I have listed some suggested resources at the end of this section that are readable by the lay person.

Allen, C. K. (1990). Encoding of Colors in Short-Term Memory. *Perceptual and Motor Skills* (71.1, 211-215).

Amabile, Teresa (1989). *Growing Up Creative*. New York: Crown Publishing.

Amabile, T. & Rovee-Collier, C. (1991, October). Contextual Variation and Memory Retrieval at Six Months. *Child Development,* 1155-66.

Ames, Carole. (1992). Classrooms: Goals, Structures, and Student Motivation. *Journal of Educational Psychology* 84, 261-71.

Ames, Carole. (1987). The Enhancement of Student Motivation. *Advances in Motivation and Achievement*. Eds. Maeher and Kleiber (Vol. 5, pgs.123-148). Greenwich, CT: JAI.

Armbruster, B. and Anderson, T. (1980). "The Effect of Mapping." *Center for the Study of Reading* 5th ed. Urbana, IL: University of Illinois.

Asbjornsen A., Hugdahl, K., & Hynd, G. W. (1990). The Effects of Head and Eye Turns on the Right Ear Advantage in Dichotic Listening. *Brain and Language* 39.3, 447-58.

Backman L., Nilsson, L. G., & Nourp, R. K. (1993). Attentional Demands and Recall of Verbal and Color Information in Action Events. *Scandinavian Journal of Psychology* 34.3, 246-254.

Bahrick, H.P. and L.K. Hall. (1991). Lifetime maintenance of high school mathematics content. J. Exp. Psychol. Gen. 120: 20-33.

Bahrick, H.P., P.C. Bahrick, and R.P. Wittlinger. (1975) Fifty years of memories for names and faces. J. Exp. Psychol. Gen. 104: 54-75.

Bartlett, J.C. and J.W. Santrock. (1979). "Affect-dependent episodic memory in young children" Child Development. 50: 513-518.

Bennett, E.L., Diamond, M.C., Krech, D., & Rosenzweig, M. (1964). Chemical and Anatomical Plasticity of the Brain. *Science*, 146, 610-619.

Benton, D., & Roberts, G. (1988). Effect of Vitamin and Mineral Supplementation on Intelligence of a Sample of School-children. *The Lancet*, 140-143.

Black J. E., et al. (1990, July). Learning Causes Synaptogenesis, Whereas Motor Activity Causes Angiogenesis, in Cerebral Cortex of Adult Rats. (Proc. of a conf. of the National Academy of Sciences). 87.14, 5568-72.

Black J. E. (1989). Effects of Complex Experience on Somatic Growth and Organ Development in Rats. *Developmental Psychobiology* 22.7, 727-52.

Block R. A., et al. (1989). Unilateral Nostril Breathing Influences Lateralized Cognitive Performance. *Brain and Cognition* 9.2, 181-90.

Bloom, et al. (1988). *Brain, Mind and Behavior*. W. H. Freeman and Co.

Boller, K. & Rovee-Collier, C. (1992). Contextual Coding and Recoding of Infant's Memories. *Journal of Experimental Child Psychology* 53.1, 1-23.

Botella, J. & Eriksen, C. W. (1992). Filtering Versus Parallel Processing in RSVP Tasks. *Perception and Psychophysics* 51.4, 334-43.

Bower, G.H. (1973). "How to ...uh...remember!" Psychology Today, 7, 63-70.

Bower, G.H. (1981). Mood and Memory. American Psychologist, 36, 129-48.

Bower, G. H. & Mann, T. (1992). Improving Recall by Recoding Interfering Material at the Time of Retrieval. *Journal of Experimental Psychology* 18.6, 1310-20.

Bower, G. H., Mann, T.D., & Morrow, G. (1990). Mental Models in Narrative Comprehension. *Science* 247.4938, 44-8.

Braun, C. M. (1992). Estimation of Interhemispheric Dynamics from Simple Unimanual Reaction Time to Extrafoveal Stimuli. *Neuropsychological Review* 3.4, 321-65.

Breier, A. Noise and Helplessness. (1988). *American Journal of Psychiatry* 144, 1419-25.

Caine, G., & Caine, R.N., Eds. (1994). Making Connections: *Teaching and the Human Brain*. Menlo Park, CA: Addison-Wesley.

Capaldi, E.J and Ian Neath. (1995). *"Remembering and Forgetting as Context Discrimination."* Learning and Memory. Volume 2, Numbers 3 and 4. 107-132.

Carpenter, G. & Grossberg, S. (1993). Normal and Amnesic Learning, Recognition and Memory by a Model of Corticohippocampal Interactions. *Trends in Neuroscience* 16.4, 131-7.

Carper, Jean. (1993). *Food: Your Miracle Medicine*. New York, NY: Harper Collins Publishers.

Carruthers, S. & Young, A. (1980). Preference of Condition Concerning Time in Learning Environments of Rural versus Eighth Grade Students. Learning Styles Network Newsletter 1.2, 1.

Christianson, S. (1992). Emotional Stress and Eyewitness Memory: A Critical Review. *Psychological Bulletin* 112.2, 284-309.

Chugani, H. T. (1991). Imaging Human Brain Development with Positron Emission Tomography. *Journal of Nuclear Medicine* 32.1, 23-6.

Clark, D.L., Kreutzberg, J.R., & Chee, F.K.W. (1977). Vestibular Stimulation Influence on Motor Development on Infants. *Science* 196, 1228-1229.

Clynes, Manfred, Ed. (1982). *Music, Mind and Brain.* New York, NY: Plenum Press.

Clynes, Manfred, Ed. (1982). Neurobiologic Functions of Rhythm, Time, and Pulse in Music. *Music, Mind and Brain.* New York, NY: Plenum Press.

Connors, Keith. (1980). *Food Additives and Hyperactive Children.* New York, NY: Plenum Press.

Connors, Keith. (1989). *Feeding the Brain.* New York, NY: Plenum Press.

Coward, Andrew. (1990). *Pattern Thinking.* New York, NY: Praeger Publishers.

Csikszentmihalyi, M. & Isabella. (1990). *Flow: The Psychology of Optimal Experience.* New York, NY: Harper & Row.

Czeisler, C. A. (1986). Arousal Cycles Can Be Reset. *Science* 233, 667-71.

Damasio, Antonio. (1994). *Descartes' Error.* New York, NY. Putnam & Sons.

Davidson, R.J. (1992). Anterior Cerebral Asymmetry and the Nature of Emotion. *Brain and Cognition* 20.1, 125-51.

Decety, J., & Ingvar, D.H. (1990). Brain Structures Participating in Mental Stimulation of Motor Behavior: A Neuropsychological Interpretation. *Acta Psychologica* 73.1,113-34.

Dekaban, A. (1970). *The Neurology of Early Childhood.* Baltimore, MD: Williams and Wilkins.

Dennison, Paul, & Dennison, Gail. (1988). *Brain Gym..* (Teacher's Ed.) Ventura, CA: Edu-kinesthetics.

Diamond, Marian. (1988). *Enriching Heredity: The Impact of the Environment on the Brain.* New York, NY: Free Press.

Dienstbier, R. (1989). Periodic Adrenaline Arousal Boosts Health, Coping. *Brain-Mind Bulletin* 14.9A.

Dixon, N. (1981). *Preconscious Processing.* New York, NY: Wiley.

Doll, W.E.J. (1989). Complexity in the Classroom. *Educational Leadership* 47.1, 65-70.

Domino, G. (1970). Interactive Effects of Achievement Orientation and Teaching Style on Academic Achievement. *ACT Research Report* 39, 1-9.

Dossey, Larry. (1993). *Healing Words.* San Francisco, CA: Harper Collins Publishers

Dunn, R. & Dunn, K. (1987). Dispelling Outmoded Beliefs About Student Learning. *Educational Leadership* 44.6, 55-61.

Dunn, Kenneth & Rita. (1992). *Bringing Out The Giftedness In Your Child*, New York, NY: John Wiley.

Dunn, R., et al. (1985). Light Up Their Lives: A Review of Research on the Effects of Lighting on Children's Achievement and Behavior. *The Reading Teacher* 38.9, 863-69.

Eich, E. (1995). "Searching for mood dependent memory" Psychology Sciences. 6: 67-75.

Emery, Charles. (1986, October). Exercise Keeps the Mind Young. *American Health.*

Engel, A. K., et al. (1992). Temporal Coding in the Visual Cortex: New Vistas on Integration in the Nervous System. *Trends in Neurosciences* 15.6, 218-26.

Epstein, H. (1974). Phrenoblysis: Special Brain and Mind Growth Periods. *Developmental Psychology* 7, 207-24.

Epstein, H. (1986). "Stages in Human Brain Development." Developmental Brain Research 30: 114-19.

Eysenck, Michael. (1994). *The Blackwell Dictionary of Cognitive Psychology.* Oxford.

Fabiani M., Karis, D., & Donchin, E. (1990). Effects of Mnemonic Strategy Manipulation in a Von Restorff Paradigm. *Electroencephalography and Clinical Neurophysiology* 75.2, 22-35.

Fitch, R.H., Brown, C.P. & Tallal, P. (1993). Left Hemisphere Specialization for Auditory Temporal Processing in Rats. *Annals of the New York Academy of Sciences* 682, 346-7.

Fox, N.A. (1991). If It's Not Left, It's Right. Electroencephalograph Asymmetry and the Development of Emotion. *American Psychologist* 46.8, 863-72.

Frederiksen, N. (1984). Implications of Cognitive Theory for Instruction in Problem-Solving. *Review of Educational Research* 54, 363-407.

Fuchs, J.L., Montemayor, M., & Greenough, W.T. (1990). Effect of Environmental Complexity on the Size of Superior Colliculus. *Behavioral and Neural Biology* 54.2, 198-203.

Galin, D., & Ornstein, R. (1974). Individual Differences in Cognitive Style: Reflexive Eye Movements. *Neuropsychologia,* 12, 367-376.

Geffen, G, J.L. Bradshaw and G. Wallace (1976). "Interhemispheric Effects on Reaction Time to Verbal and Nonverbal Visual Stimuli," Journal of Experimental Psychology 87 415-422.

Goldman, J., et al. (1986). Behavioral Effects of Sucrose on Preschool Children. *Journal of Abnormal Child Psychology* 14, 565-78.

Goleman, Daniel. (1995). *Emotional Intelligence:* Bantam Books, NY.

Gordon, H.W. (1978). Left Hemisphere Dominance for Rhythmic Elements in Dichotically Presented melodies. *Cortex* 14, 58-76.

Gratton, G., Coles, M. G., & Donchin, E. (1992). Optimizing the Use of Information: Strategic Control of Activation of Responses. *Journal of Experimental Psychology* 121.4, 480-506.

Greenough, W.T., & Anderson, B.J. (1991). Cerebellar Synaptic Plasticity: Relation to Learning Versus Neural Activity. *Annals of the New York Academy of Science* 627, 231-47.

Greenough, W.T., and B. Anderson. (1991). Cerebellar Synaptic Plasticity. *Annals of the New York Academy of Sciences* 627, 231-47.

Greenough, W.T., Withers, G. & Anderson, B. (1992). Experience-Dependent Synaptogenesis as a Plausible Memory Mechanism. *Learning and Memory: The Behavioral and Biological Substrates.* (Gormezano, I. & Wasserman, E., Eds.) Hillsdale, NJ: Erlbaum & Associates. pp. 209-29.

Grolnick, W.S. & Ryan, R.M. (1987). Autonomy in Children's Learning: An Experimental and Individual Difference Investigation. *Journal of Personality and Social Psychology* 52, 890-898.

Grunwald, L., & Goldberg, J. (1993, July). Babies Are Smarter Than You Think. *Life Magazine,* 45-60.

Gur, R.E., Gur, R.C., & Harris, L.J. (1975). Cerebral Activation as Measured by Subject's Eye Movements. *Neuropsychologia,* 13, 35-44.

Hampson, E. & Kimura, D. (1988). Reciprocal Effects of Hormonal Fluctuations on Human Motor and Perceptual Spatial Skills. *Behavioral Neuroscience* 102.3, 456-9.

Hannaford, Carla. (1995). *Smart Moves.* Great Ocean Publishing Co. Arlington, VA.

Harper, A.E., & Peters, J.C. (1989). Protein Intake, Brain Amino Acid and Serotonin Concentration and Protein Self-Selection. *Journal of Nutrition* 119.5, 677-89.

Harth, Erich. (1995). *The Creative Loop.* Addison-Wesley, Reading, MA.

Hassler, M. (1991). Testosterone and Musical Talent. *Experimental and Clinical Endocrinology* 98.2, 89-98.

Healy, Alice & Lyle Bourne. (1995). *Learning and Memory of Knowledge and Skills.* Thousand Oaks, CA. Sage Publications.

Healy, J. (1990). *Endangered Minds: Why Our Children Can't Think.* New York, NY: Simon and Schuster.

Healy, J. (1995). *Your Child's Growing Mind.* New York, NY: Doubleday.

Hermann, D.J. & Hanwood, J.R. (1980). More evidence for the Existence of the Separate Semantic and Episodic Stores in Long-Term Memory. Journal of Experimental Psychology: Human Learning and Memory 6 & 5, 467-478.

Hirsch, A. (1993). Floral Odor Increases Learning Ability. Presentation at annual conference of American Academy of Neurological & Orthopedic Surgery. Contact: Allan Hirsch, Smell & Taste Treatment Foundation, Chicago, IL.

Hobson, J.A. (1989). *Sleep.* New York, NY: W.H. Freeman.

Hobson, J.A. (1995). The Chemistry of Consciousness

Hopfield, J., Feinstein, D., & Palmer, R. (1983, July). Unlearning Has a Stabilizing Effect in Collective Memories. *Nature.* pp. 158-59.

Horn, G. (1991). Learning, Memory and the Brain. *Indian Journal of Physiology and Pharmacology* 35.1, 3-9.

Horne J. (1989). Sleep Loss and Divergent Thinking Ability. *Sleep* 11.6, 528-36.

Horne J. (1992, October 15). Human Slow Wave Sleep: A Review and Appraisal of Recent Findings, with Implications for Sleep Functions and Psychiatric Illness. *Experientia* pp. 941-54.

Howard, Pierce. (1994). *Owners Manual for the Brain.* Leornian Press: Austin, Texas.

Huchinson, Michael. (1986). *Megabrain.* New York, NY: Beech Tree Books.

Huttenlocher, P.R. (1990). Morphometric Study of Human Cerebral Cortex Development. *Neuropsychologia* 28.6, 517-27.

Iaccino, James. (1993). *Left Brain-Right Brain Differences: Inquiries, Evidence, and New Approaches.* Hillsdale, NJ: Lawrence Erlbaum & Associates.

Introini-Collision, I.B., Miyazaki, B. & McGaugh, J.L. (1991). Involvement of the Amygdala in the Memory-Enhancing Effects of Clenbuterol. *Psychopharmacology* 104.4, 541-4.

Isaacs, K.R., et al. (1992). Exercise and the Brain: Angiogenesis in the Adult Rat Cerebellum After Vigorous Physical Activity and Motor Skill Learning. *Journal of Cerebral Blood Flow and Metabolism* 12.1, 110-9.

Jacobs, B., Schall, M. & Scheibel, A.B. (1993). A Quantitative Dendritic Analysis of Wernicke's Area in Humans: Gender, Hemispheric and Environmental Factors. *Journal of Comparative Neurology* 327.1, 97-111.

Jenkins, D.J., et al. (1989). Nibbling Versus Gorging: Metabolic Advantages of Increased Meal Frequency. *New England Journal of Medicine* 321.14, PGS. 929-34.

Jensen, Eric. (1994). *The Learning Brain.* Del Mar, CA: Turning Point Publishing.

Jensen, Eric. (1995). *Brain-Based Learning & Teaching.* Del Mar, CA: Turning Point Publishing.

Jernigan, T.L., & Tallal, P. (1990). Late Childhood Changes in Brain Morphology Observable with MRI. *Developmental Medicine and Child Neurology* 32.5, 379-85.

Kandel, M. & Kandel, E. (1994, May). Flights of Memory. *Discover Magazine,* 32-38.

Kandel, E. & Hawkins, R. (1992, September). The Biological Basis of Learning and Individuality. *Scientific American* pp. 79-86.

Kanter, R.M., Clark, D.L., Allen, L.C., & Chase, M.F. (1976). Effects of Vestibular Stimulation on Nystagmus Response and Motor Performance in the Developmentally Delayed Infant. *Physical Therapy,* 54:(4), 414-21.

Kaplan, R. (1983). Reader's Visual Fields Increase with Color Therapy. *Brain Mind Bulletin* 8.14F.

Kenyon, Thomas. (1994). *Brain States.* Naples, FL: U.S. Publishing.

Kesner, R.P. (1983). "Mnemonic Functions of the Hippocampus: Correspondence between Animals and Humans" Conditioning Representation of Neural Function, ed. C.D.Woody (New York: Plenum Press).

Khalsa, D., Ziegler, M., & Kennedy, B. (1986). Body Sides Switch Dominance. *Life Sciences* 38, 1203-14.

Klutky, N. (1990). Sex Differences in Memory Performance for Odors, on Sequences and Colors. *Zeitscrift fur Experimentelle und Angewandte Psychologie* 37.3, 437-46.

Kohn, A. (1994). Punished by Rewards. Houghton-Mifflin. Boston, MA

Kopera, H. (1980). Female Hormones and Brain Function. *Hormones and the Brain.* (de Wied & Van Keep, Eds.) Lancaster, England: MTP Press. pp. 189-203.

Kosmarskaya, E.N. (1963). The Influence of Peripheral Stimuli on Development of Nerve Cells. [In The Development of the Brain and its Disturbance by Harmful Factors, Klosovski, B.N., Ed.] New York, NY: Macmillan Publishing.

Kosslyn, Steven. (1988). Wet Mind. Simon & Schuster. New York, NY.

Kotulak, Ronald. Unraveling Hidden Mysteries of the Brain. (1993, 11-16 April). *Chicago Tribune.*

LeDoux, J., & Hirst, W. (1986). Attention. *Mind and Brain: Dialogues in Cognitive Neuroscience.* New York, NY: Cambridge. pp. 105-85.

LeDeoux, J.E. (1989). "Cognitive-Emotional Interactions in the Brain," Cognition and Emotion: 3 pgs.267-89.

Lenneberg, E.H. (1967). Biological Foundations of Language. New York: Wiley & Sons.

Lepper, M.R. (1981). Intrinsic and Extrinsic Motivation in Children: Detrimental Effects of Superfluous Social Controls. W.A. Collins, Ed.] Aspects of the Development of Competence: The Minnesota Symposium on Child Psychology. Vol 14. Hillsdale, NJ: Lawrence Erlbaum. pp. 155-214.

Levine, S.C., Jordan, N.C., & Huttenlocher, J. (1992). Development of Calculation Abilities in Young Children. *Journal of Experimental Child Psychology* 53.1, Ú72-103.

Levy, J. (1983). Research Synthesis on Right and Left Hemispheres: We Think With Both Sides of the Brain. *Educational Leadership* 40.4, 66-71.

Lewicki, P., Hill, T., & Czyzewska, M. (1992). Nonconscious Acquisition of Information. *American Psychologist* 47.6, 796-801.

Lieberman, H.R., Wurtman, J.J., & Teicher, M.H. (1989). Circadian Rhythms in Healthy Young and Elderly Humans. *Neurobiology of Aging* 10.3, 259-65.

Loftus, E.F and G.R. Loftus (1980). "On the permanance of stored information in the brain" American Psychology. 35: 409-20.

Luiten, J., Ames, W., & Ackerson, G. (1980). A Meta-Analysis of the Effects of Advance Organizers on Learning and Retention. *American Educational Research Journal* 17, 211-18.

Michaud, Ellen. (1991). Boost Your Brain Power. Rodal Press, Emmaus, PA.

Maguire, J. (1990). *Care and Feeding of the Brain.* New York, NY: Doubleday.

Malone, T., & Lepper, M. (1987). Making Learning Fun: A Semanticomy of Intrinsic Motivations for Learning. *Aptitude, Learning and Instruction III: Cognitive and Affective Process Analyses.* (Snow & Farr, Eds.) Hillsdale, NJ: Lawrence Erlbaum & Assoc. pp. 223-53.

Mandler, G. (1983). The Nature of Emotions. *States of Mind.* (Miller. J., Ed.) New York, NY: Pantheon Books.

Mark, Vernon. (1989). *Brain Power.* Boston, MA: Houghton-Mifflin.

Marzolla, Jean & Lloyd, Janice. (1972). *Learning Through Play.* New York, NY: Harper & Row.

Martin, R.C. (1993). Short-Term Memory and Sentence Processing: Evidence from Neuropsychology. *Memory and Cognition* 21.2 , 176-83.

Matthews, R.C. (1977). Semantic judgements as encoding operations: The effects of attention to particular semantic categories on the usefulness of interitem relations in recall. J. of Exper. Psychology: Human Learning and Memory, 3, 160-73.

McGaugh J.L. (1989). Dissociating Learning and Performance: Drug and Hormone Enhancement of Memory Storage. *Brain Research Bulletin* 23.4-5, 339-45.

McGaugh J.L., et al. (1990). Involvement of the Amygdaloid Complex in Neuromodulatory Influences on Memory Storage. *Neuroscience and Biobehavioral Reviews* 14.4, 425-31.

McGee, M. (1979). Human Spatial Abilities: Psychometric Studies and Environmental, Genetic, Hormonal and Neurological Influences. *Psychological Bulletin* 86.5, 889-918.

McGuiness, D. (1985).*When Children Don't Learn.* New York, NY: Basic Books.

Meese, J.L., Wigfield, A., & Eccles, J.S. (1990). Predictors of Math Anxiety and its Influence on Young Adolescents' Course Enrollment Intentions and Performance in Mathematics. *Journal of Educational Psychology* 82, 60-70.

Michaud, E., & Wild, R. (1991). *Boost Your Brain Power.* Emmaus, PA: Rodale Press.

Milich, R., & Pelham, W.E. (1986). The Effects of Sugar Ingestion on the Classroom and Playgroup Behavior. *Journal of Consulting & Clinical Psychology* 54, 1-5.

Mills, R.C. (1987, April). Relationship Between School Motivational Climate, Teacher Attitudes, Student Mental Health, School Failure and Health Damaging Behavior. (Paper at Annual Conference of the American Educational Research Association). Washington, D.C.

Mills, L. & Rollman, G.B. (1980). Hemispheric Asymmetry for Auditory Perception of Temporal Order. *Neuropsychologia,* 18, 41-47.

Minsky, Marvin. (1986). *The Society of Mind.* Touchstone/Simon & Schuster, New York.

Morris, P.E. & Cook, N. (1978). "When do first letter mnemonics aid recall?" British Journal of Educational Psychology, 48, 22-8.

Nadel, L. (1990). Varieties of Spatial Cognition. Psychobiological Considerations. *Annals of the New York Academy of Sciences* 608, 613-26.

Nakamura, K. (1993). A Theory of Cerebral Learning Regulated by the Reward System. *Biological Cybernetics* 68.6, 491-8.

Neisser, Ulric & Harsch, Nicole. (1992). Phantom Flashbulbs: False recollections of hearing the news about Challenger. [In *Affect and Accuracy in Recall: Studies of "flashbulb" memories*] Cambridge University (Winograd, E. & Neisser, U., Eds.)

Nummela, R., & Rosengren, T. (1986). What's Happening in Student's Brain's May Redefine Teaching. *Educational Leadership* 43.8, 49-53.

Nummela, R., & Rosengren, T. The Brain's Routes and Maps: Vital Connections in Learning. *NAASP Bulletin* 72: 83-86.

Oakhill, J. (1988). Time of Day Affects Aspects of Memory. *Applied Cognitive Psychology* 2, 203-12.

O'Keefe, J., & Nadel, L. (1978). *The Hippocampus as a Cognitive Map.* Oxford, England: Clarendon Press.

Olds, James. (1992). Mapping the Mind onto the Brain. *The Neurosciences: Paths of Discovery.* (Worden, F., Swazey, J., & Adelman, G., Eds.) Boston, MA: Birkhauser.

Orlock, Carol. (1993). *Inner Time.* New York, NY: Birch Lane Press, Carol Publishing.

Ostrander, Sheila & Schroeder, Lynn. (1991). *SuperMemory.* New York, NY: Carroll & Graf Publishers.

Overton, D.A. (1984). State-dependent learning and drug discrimations. In L.L. Iverson, S.D. Iverson, S.H. Snyder (Eds.), Handbook of Psychopharmacology (Vol 18) pgs. 59-127. New York: Plenum.

Pelton, Ross. (1989). *Mind Food & Smart Pills.* New York, NY: Bantam Doubleday.

Pfurtscheller, G. & Berghold, A. (1989). Patterns of Cortical Activation During Planning of Voluntary Movement. *Electroencephalography and Clinical Neurophysiology* 72, 250-58.

Pribram, K.H. and McGuiness, D. (1975). "Arousal, Activation and Effort in the Control of Attention." Psychological Review 82: 116-149.

Price, G. (1980). Which Learning Style Elements are Stable and Which Tend to Change? *Learning Styles Network Newsletter* 4.2, 38-40.

Pulvirenti, L. (1992). Neural Plasticity and Memory: Towards an Integrated View. *Functional Neurology* 7.6, 49-57.

Restak, R. (1988). *The Brain.* New York, NY: Warner Books.

Rice, R. (1975). The Effects of Tactile-Kinesthetic Stimulation on the Subsequent Development of Premature Infants. (Unpublished doctoral dissertation) University of Texas at Austin. *Dissertation Abstracts* 35(5): 2148B.

Robin, D.E., & Shortridge, R.T., (1979). Lateralization of Tumors of the Nasal Cavity and Paranasal Sinuses and its Relation to Etiology. *Lancet* 8118, 695-696.

Roederer, Juan. (1981). Physical and Neuropsychological Foundations of Music. *Music, Mind and Brain.* (Clynes, Manfred, Ed.) New York, NY: Plenum Press.

Roland, P., et. al. (1990). Functional Anatomy of Storage, Recall and Recognition of a Visual Pattern in Man. Neuroreport: An *International Journal for the Rapid Communication of Research in Neuroscience* 1.1, 53-6.

Rose, F., Davey, M., & Attree, E. (1993). How Does Environmental Enrichment Aid Performance Following Cortical Injury in the Rat? *Neuroreport: An International Journal for the Rapid Communication of Research in Neuroscience* 4.2, 163-6.

Rose, Steven. (1992). *The Making of Memory.* New York, NY. Anchor/Doubleday.

Rosenberg, B.A., (1980). Mental Task Instruction and Optokinetic Nystagmus to the Left and Right. *Journal of Experimental Psychology: Human Perception and Performance,* 6, 459-472.

Rosenfield, I. (1988). *The Invention of Memory.* New York, NY: Basic Books.

Rosenfield, M., & Gilmartin, B. (1990). Effect of Target Proximity on the Open-Loop Accommodative Response. *Optometry and Vision Science* 67.2, 74-9.

Rosenfield, M., & Gilmartin, B., & Ciuffreda, K.J. (1991). Effect of Surround Propinquity on the Open-Loop Accommodative Response. *Investigative Ophthalmology and Visual Science* 32.1, 142-7.

Rosenzweig, M.R., Love, W. & Bennett, E.L. (1968). Effects of a Few Hours a Day of Enriched Experience on Brain Chemistry and Brain Weights. *Physiology and Behavior* 3:819-825.

Rosenzweig, M.R., Krech, D., Bennett, E.L., & Diamond, M.C. (1962). Effects of Environmental Complexity and Training on Brain Chemistry and Anatomy. *Journal of Comparative Physiological Psychology* 55(4): 429-437.

Ross, E.D. (1984). Right Hemisphere's Role in Language, Affective Behavior and Emotion. *Trends in Neuroscience* 7, 342-345.

Rossi, A.S., & Rossi, P.E. (1980). Body Time and Social Time: Mood Patterns by Cycle Phase and Day of the Week. *The Psychobiology of Sex Differences and Sex Roles.* (Parsons, J.E., Ed.) London, England: Hemisphere. pp. 269-301.

Rossi, A.S., & Rossi, P.E. (1986). Hemispheric Dominance Switches.

Rossi, E.L. & Nimmons, D. (1991). The 20-Minute Break: Using the New Science of Ultradian Rhythms. Los Angeles: Tarcher.

Schab, F.R. (1990). "Odors and the remembrance of things past" Journal of Experimental Psychology, Learning, Memory and Cognition 16: 648-655.

Schacter, D.L. (1992). Understanding Implicit Memory. *American Psychologist* 47.4, 559-69.

Schatz, C.J. (1990). Impulse Activity and the Patterning of Connections During CNS Development. *Neuron* 5.6, 745-56.

Schatz, C.J. (1992, September). The Developing Brain. *Scientific American.* pp. 60-7.

Scheibel, Arnold. (1994, November 1). You Can Continuously Improve Your Mind and Your Memory. *Bottom Line Personal* (15) 21, pgs..9-10.

Schneider, W. (1993). Varieties of Working Memory As Seen in Biology and in Connectionist/Control Architectures. *Memory and Cognition* 21.2, 184-92.

Schunk, D.H. (1990). Goal-Setting and Self-Efficacy During Self-Regulated Learning. *Educational Psychologist* 25.1, 71-86.

Schwartz, J & Tallal, P. (1980). Rate of Acoustic Change May Underlie Hemispheric Specialization for Speech Perception. *Science* 207, 1380-1381.

Segal, J., Chipman, S., & Glaser, R. (1985). *Thinking and Learning Skills.* Vol. I.

Silverstein, Alvin, & Silverstein, Virginia. (1986). *The World of the Brain.* New York, NY: Morrow Jr. Books.

Sirevaag, A.M., & Greenough, W.T. (1991). Plasticity of GFAP-Immunoreactive Astrocyte Size and Number in Visual Cortex of Rats Reared in Complex Environments. *Brain Research* 540.1-2, 273-8.

Smith, A.P., Kendrick, A.M., & Maben, A. (1992). Effects of Caffeine on Performance and Mood in the Late Morning and After Lunch. *Neuropsychobiology* 26.4, 198-204.

Smith, B.D., Davidson, R.A., & Green, R.L. (1993). Effects of Caffeine and Gender on Physiology and Performance: Further Tests on a Biobehavioral Model. *Physiology and Behavior* 54.3, 415-22.

Soloveichik, Simon. (1979, May). Odd Way to Teach, But It Works. *Soviet Life Magazine.*

Squire, L. (1992). Memory and the Hippocampus: A Synthesis from Findings with Rats, Monkeys and Humans. *Psychological Review* 99.2, 195-231.

Squire, L. (1995). Mystery of Memory. Article in San Diego Union Newspaper. 5/10/95. pp. E-1-4

Sternberg, Robert. Beyond I.Q.: *A Triarchical Theory of Human Intelligence.*

Sullivan, R.M., McGaugh, J.L. & Leon, M. (1991). Norepinephrine-Induced Plasticity and One-Trial Olfactory Learning in Neonatal Rats. *Brain Research* 60.2, 219-28.

Sutter, Alice. (1991, January). VDT Noise Causes Stress. *Issues in Human Resources.*

Sylwester, R. (1995). *A Celebration of Neurons.* ASCD. Alexandria, VA.

Tallal, P. (1991). Hormonal Influences in Developmental Learning Disabilities. *Psychoneuroendocrinology* 16.1-3, 203-11.

Tallal, P., Miller, S., & Fitch, R.H. (1993). Neurobiological Basis for Speech: a Case for the Preeminence of Temporal Processing. *Annals of the New York Academy of Sciences* 682, 27-47.

Thal, D.J., & Tobias, S. (1992). Communicative Gestures in Children with Delayed Onset of Oral Expressive Vocabulary. *Journal of Speech and Hearing Research* 35.6, 1281-9.

Thal, D.J., & Tobias, S., & Morrison, D. (1991). Language and Gesture in Late Talkers: A 1-Year Follow-Up. *Journal of Speech and Hearing Research* 34.3, 604-12.

Thayer, R. (1986). Time of Day Affects Energy Levels. *Brain-Mind Bulletin* 12, 3D.

Thayer, R. (1989). *The Biopsychology of Mood and Arousal.* New York, NY: Oxford University Press.

Thompson, Richard. (1993). *The Brain.* W.H. Freeman and Company. New York.

Trautman, P. (1979). An Investigation of the Relationship Between Selected Instructional Techniques and Identified Cognitive Style. *Dissertation.* St. John's University.

Treisman, A. & Gormican, S. (1988). Feature Analysis in Early Vision: Evidence from Search Asymmetries. *Psychological Review* 95, 15-48.

Trevarthen, Colin. (1972). Brain Bisymmetry and the Role of the Corpus Callosum in Behavior and Conscious Experience. [In *Cerebral Interhemispheric Relations*] Bratislavia, Czechoslovakia: Publishing House of the Slovak Academy of Sciences.

Trevarthen, Colin. (1990). Growth and Education of the Hemispheres. *Brain Circuits and Functions of the Mind: Essays in Honor of Roger W. Sperry.* (Trevarthen, Colwyn, Ed.) New York, NY: Cambridge University Press.

Tryphonas, H., & Trites, R. (1979). Food Allergy in Children with Hyperactivity. *Annals of Allergy* 42, 22-7.

Tulving, E. (1985). How many memory systems are there? American Psychologist, 40, 385-98.

Uhl, F., et al. (1990). Cerebral Correlates of Imagining Colors, Faces and a Map - Negative Cortical DC Potentials. *Neuropsychologia* 28.1, 81-93.

Unger, Georges. (1976). Biochemistry of Intelligence. *Research Communications in Psychology, Psychiatry & Behavior* 1.5-6, 597-606.

Urban, M.J. (1992). Auditory Subliminal Stimulation: A Re-examination. *Perceptual and Motor Skills* 74.2, 515-41.

Vincent, J-D. (1990). *The Biology of Emotions.* Cambridge, MA: Basil Blackwell.

Wallace, C. S., et al. (1992). Increases in Dendritic Length in Occipital Cortex After 4 Days of Differential Housing in Weanling Rats. *Behavioral and Neural Biology* 58.1, 64-8.

Webb, D., & Webb, T. (1990). *Accelerated Learning with Music.* Norcross, GA: Accelerated Learning Systems.

Weingartner, H and L.A. Failace. (1971). "Alcohol state-dependent learning in man." Journal of Nervous Mental Disorders. 153: 395-406.

Wenger, Win. (1992). *Beyond Teaching & Learning.* Singapore. Project Renaissance.

Wenger, Win. (1995). The Einstein Factor.

White, R.T. (1980). An Investigation of the Relationship Between Selected Instructional Methods and Selected Elements of Emotional Learning Style Upon Student Achievement in Seventh-Grade Social Studies. *Unpublished Dissertation.* St John's University.

Wilson, D.A., Willnre, J., Kurz, E.M., & Nadel, L. (1986). Early Handling Increases Hippocampal Long-Term Potentiation in Young Rats. Behavioral Brain Research, 21, 223-227.

Wittrock, M.C., Ed. (1977). *The Human Brain.* Englewood Cliffs, NJ: Prentice-Hall.

Wlodkowski, R. (1985). *Enhancing Adult Motivation to Learn.* San Francisco, CA: Jossey-Bass Publishers.

Wurtman, J. *Managing Your Mind & Mood Through Food.* New York, NY: Harper/Collins, 1986.

Wurtman, J. (1988). *Dietary Phenyalanine and Brain Function.* Boston, MA: Birkhauser. p. 374.

Wurtman, R.J. (1990). Carbohydrate Craving. *Drugs* Supplement 39.3, 49-52.

Wurtman, R.J., & Ritter-Walker, E. (1988). *Dietary Phenylanine and Brain Function.* Boston: Birkhauser.

Suggested Resources for Additional Reading

Books on Learning, Teaching, and the Brain

The Brain Store™ features countless books, posters, CDs, and brain-related products. This innovative education resource company is all about the science of learning. You'll find resources for:

- Teaching and Training
- Music and Dance
- Enrichment
- Organizational Change
- Staff Development
- Early Childhood

To view all of our products, log on at: **www.thebrainstore.com**, or call (800) 325-4769 or (858) 546-7555 for a <u>FREE</u> color resource catalog.

The LearningBrain Newsletter

Get timely research-based articles on a monthly basis. Log on to our online newsletter and stay abreast of the newest and most relevant information on topics like cognition, environment, nutrition, arts, memory, school policy, mind-body, and fragile brains. Save hundreds of hours in research time and expense. Gain twenty-first century teaching and training strategies. To get a free sample issue, log on at: **www.learningbrain.com** or call (800) 325-4769 or (858) 546-7555.

Conference: *Learning Brain Expo®*

A world-class gathering featuring more than fifty renowned speakers on the brain and learning. Session topics include music, movement, early childhood, emotions, memory, the fragile brain, and brain imaging. Get dozens of practical ideas and network with like-minded professionals. This enriching event is held twice a year. For more information, log on at: **www.brainexpo.com**, or call (800) 325-4769 or (858) 546-7555.

Free Samples

Go to **www.thebrainstore.com** to get free tips, tools, and strategies. You'll also find selected products at 40 percent savings. In addition, many books offer you a sneak online preview of the table of contents and sample pages, so you'll know before you order if it's for you. At The Brain Store™, online shopping is safe, quick, and easy!

Meet the Author

Eric Jensen is a visionary educator who is committed to making a positive, significant, and lasting difference in the way we learn. He's a member of the prestigious Society for Neuroscience and New York Academy of Sciences. A former middle-school teacher and college instructor, Jensen is the author of more than a dozen books on learning and teaching. He co-founded the world's first experimental brain-compatible academic enrichment program in 1982 that now has more than 30,000 graduates. Currently, he's a staff developer and consultant living in San Diego, California.

Other Books by Eric Jensen

Super Teaching, Learning Smarter, The Learning Brain, Brain-Based Learning, Trainer's Bonanza, Teaching with the Brain in Mind, Joyful Fluency (with Lynn Dhority), *The Great Memory Book* (with Karen Markowitz), *Learning with the Body in Mind, Music with the Brain in Mind,* and *Different Brains, Different Learners.* Available through The Brain Store™. Log on at: **www.thebrainstore.com**, or call (800) 325-4769 or (858) 546-7555.

Author Contact

Fax (858) 642-0404 or e-mail at eric@jlcbrain.com

Trainings Facilitated by Eric Jensen

"Teaching with the Brain in Mind" is a 6-day workshop for teachers, trainers, and other change agents with a focus on the brain, how we learn, and how to boost achievement.

"The Fragile Brain" is a 3-day program for teachers, special educators, counselors, and other change agents with a focus on what can go wrong with the learner's brain and how to treat it.

For registration information, dates, and costs call (888) 638-7246 or fax (858) 642-0404.

Notes:

Notes: